Reclaim Yourself

A Memoir of Strength, Survival, and Starting Over

Camee Adams

Finesse Literary Press Ltd.

Copyright © 2025 by Camee Adams.

All rights reserved.

No portion of this book may be reproduced in any form without written permission from the publisher or author, except as permitted by U.S. copyright law.

This publication is designed to provide accurate and authoritative information in regard to the subject matter covered. It is sold with the understanding that neither the author nor the publisher is engaged in rendering legal, investment, accounting or other professional services. While the publisher and author have used their best efforts in preparing this book, they make no representations or warranties with respect to the accuracy or completeness of the contents of this book and specifically disclaim any implied warranties of merchantability or fitness for a particular purpose. No warranty may be created or extended by sales representatives or written sales materials. The advice and strategies contained herein may not be suitable for your situation. You should consult with a professional when appropriate. Neither the publisher nor the author shall be liable for any loss of profit or any other commercial damages, including but not limited to special, incidental, consequential, personal, or other damages. The events and conversations are recounted to the best of the author's memory. Some names and identifying details have been changed to protect the privacy of individuals. Any resemblance to real people, living or dead, is purely coincidental unless explicitly stated.

First edition 2025, published by Finesse Literary Press Ltd.

Contents

1. How Life Started - Full of Love, Peace and Adventure — 1
2. Disconnection from Self — 20
3. Confusion — 25
4. The News That Changed The Course of My Life Forever — 38
5. The Reason for My Divorce Will Always Be Coercive Control and Domestic Violence. — 65
6. 3 a.m. Phone Call — 115
7. Court Proceedings and Being Done for Good — 130
8. Starting to Feel Like Myself Again — 139
9. Getting Stronger, Fighting, Fitness — 154
10. Heartbreak — 174
11. Professional Athlete Status — 191
12. Where We Are Now — 198

Acknowledgements — 204

Chapter 1
How Life Started - Full of Love, Peace and Adventure

Before I knew the weight of the world, I knew the weight of rain: constant, gentle, and always there. Oregon was more than a home; it was a quiet, peaceful symphony of towering trees, moss-covered sidewalks, and mist that blurred the edges of memory.

I'd watch fat slugs cling to the entryway glass after rainy days. The air was always filled with the fragrance of rhododendrons and rose bushes from our yard, and towering neighborhood trees offered the perfect setting for weekly tree-climbing adventures, where I could escape into my own world and feel free. I'd walk to school most mornings in a gentle drizzle, never needing an umbrella unless it was pouring. And I'd pick raspberries off the neighbor's bushes on the way home.

To this day, rain still takes me back to those simple, magical days.

CAMEE ADAMS

In Oregon, our closest friends and neighbors were a family with four daughters, each with a traditional Irish name starting with "S". Their home was cozy, brimming with love, plants, and antique treasures. The backyard playhouse was a world of its own, full of imagination, laughter, and the occasional daddy longlegs while their back door was always open, making their house feel like an extension of our own.

The youngest "S" sister, Shauna, was my best friend, even though she was a little older. We became the self-proclaimed birdwatching experts of our neighborhood, armed with nothing but whistles, binoculars, and an unshakable confidence that could've convinced anyone we were *totally* qualified. We'd sit outside, eyes glued to the feeders, enthusiastically scribbling down notes about our sightings. Never mind that our birdwatching techniques were more like screeching our whistles and looking up birds in our books, but our enthusiasm was unstoppable.

To this day, I get a ridiculous amount of joy whenever I spot a Chickadee. And over the years, certain birds have become little symbols of love and physical testaments in faith for me because who wouldn't want a cute little feathered friend to represent something so meaningful and loving?

Shuana and I were also passionate about gymnastics. We got matching short haircuts, and by second grade, we were throwing double backflips with a spot. Shauna had grace and elegance, while I was all about strength and intensity. Even at that age, the long hours in the gym weren't just about training—they left me feeling accomplished, focused, connected, and strong, laying an early foundation for the sport that would later change my life and transform me into the woman I am today.

After a few wonderful years in Oregon, my parents made the big announcement: We were moving to Utah. My dad had a new job offer, and while we were thrilled about the idea of living near mountains and experiencing four seasons, the thought of saying goodbye to our best friends weighed on our young hearts. My dad left first to get settled while my mom stayed behind to sell the house and finish out the school year with us. During those last months, we lived across the street with them, furnishing their unfinished attic into little cozy corners of our own. It was a bittersweet time, full of laughter and fun, but also we knew the change was coming. When the day finally arrived to pack up and head to Utah, it felt like a tug-of-war between excitement for the adventure ahead and heartache over leaving so much behind. But we loaded up the moving van and road tripped across states to start our new life.

The road trip from Oregon to Utah was thirteen hours of highways, snacks, and music, but one of our favorite memories from the trip is when we stopped at a gas station and changed into our pajamas right there in the bathroom. It felt silly and spontaneous, like something out of a movie. We were tired, a little delirious, and laughing as we swapped jeans for cozy pj's under the gas station's bathroom fluorescent lights.

That quick outfit change somehow shifted the whole energy; it turned the long, tiring haul into something that felt like an adventure. After we changed, everything felt lighter, more fun, and just a little bit magical. It was one of those small, unexpected moments I'll carry with me forever, the kind that makes me smile every time I think of it.

My mom had a gift for that, of turning the hard stuff into something memorable, of making even the most exhausting moments feel special.

Road trips and cozy pajamas remind me of love.

That first year, Utah saw record-breaking snowfall, a shock compared to Oregon, where even a trace of snow could close schools. Here, three feet didn't faze anyone. My siblings and I spent that first winter building snow forts, having snowball fights, sledding, and, on special days, being pulled behind our dad's Ford Explorer on a sled—a wild, mostly unsafe, but unforgettable thrill learned and handed down from his small-town roots.

Now that we were in Utah, my dad was determined that we'd learn to ski. After all, the state is known for the best snow on Earth, right? I'm not sure if it was his love for the outdoors and wanting us to be part of the culture, to give my mom a break, or if he was looking forward to creating new family memories, but that winter, we'd cram into the Ford with all of our ski gear, snacks, and *questionable* enthusiasm. Then we'd head up to Snowbird, Alta, or Brighton.

We created some fun memories over the years, but one particular trip still stands out.

Looking back, not every ski trip went exactly as planned, but those are usually the ones you remember most.

RECLAIM YOURSELF

Sometimes, the canyons going up to the ski resorts got shut down on heavy snow days, but that morning, my dad decided *we were making it up there no matter what.* The snow was coming down sideways in a full-on whiteout blizzard, but somehow, we made it to the top. Victory! Or so we thought.

We parked the Explorer, layered up like marshmallows, strapped on our skis, and set off into the storm. If you've been skiing, you know there are two types of days: sunny and glorious or absolute survival mode. This was the latter. Visibility? Nonexistent. Goggles? Not for us. My dad, in his infinite wisdom, decided goggles were for amateurs and took us straight to a blue run because why not spice things up with a challenge, right? After all, we were his kids, which meant we were all physically capable and adventurous, but things got chaotic fast. My dad quickly realized this might have been an oversight and took my younger brother back down the mountain to buy goggles. That's when it happened.

Somehow, my sister and I ended up on a Black Diamond run **with moguls**. For context, a Black Diamond is the advanced run—the place you go when you're ready to test the limits of your skiing skills. We were still beginners, barely managing green runs, and suddenly, we were staring down a mountain of frozen death humps.

My sister remembers this moment vividly: me going downhill like a human torpedo, bouncing off moguls like I was in a washing machine on the spin cycle, completely out of control. I remember clenching every muscle in sheer panic, praying I'd live to see another day while miraculously making it through the moguls. I still don't know how I made it.

We were flying down that mountain at speeds previously unknown to beginner skiers, flailing, bouncing, trying to pizza our skies, shrieking the entire way. At some point, we lost our skis, which, in hindsight, was probably a blessing. We had to hike the rest of the way down, looking like exhausted escapees from a blizzard disaster movie, still processing what just happened. To this day, we have gut-busting belly laughs about that experience.

Our dad may not have planned it, but that chaotic ski adventure was just one of many times he unknowingly taught us a valuable life lesson: sometimes, you've just got to push through and get er' done.

Whether it was surviving a mogul-filled mountain, tackling chores we didn't want to do, or finishing tough jobs or sports practices, our dad's insistence on hard work became a family motto that shaped our childhood.

I didn't know that a new kind of chaos would enter my life in a few short years—one that would shatter my innocence, leave wounds on my soul, and lead me down a path that would take years to find my way back from.

My Mom

Growing up in a small town, my mom has a free spirit that sets her apart—a unique blend of warmth, creativity, spunk, and that salt-of-the-earth sincerity. She has a natural gift for thinking of others in thoughtful, meaningful ways that make everyone around her feel cared for. She can still pull off her high school cheerleading cheers with ease, a joyful reminder of the energy and spirit she's always carried. And though she may never speak of it, she has quietly sat with more people in their hardest moments than anyone will ever know – offering comfort and peace. She has a heart that never stops giving.

My mom is the kind of woman who gave her whole heart and life to her children. It was a hallmark of her generation, sacrificing personal identity in favor of motherhood in a society that often overlooked a woman's sense of self outside her family. She loved us deeply, cared for us unconditionally, and gave endlessly, even as she quietly struggled to define a life of her own outside of motherhood.

When you're a child, you only see your mom as *Mom*. But as an adult, you begin to see her as a woman—a whole person with her own dreams, struggles, and strengths. And now, I see her clearly: the most kind, hardworking, loyal, and selfless woman I know, and I'm not just saying that because she's my mother.

She worked outside the home for my entire childhood and adult life. My siblings and I would call her at work with silly questions: *Can we ride our bikes to the pool? Can we eat the popsicles in the freezer? When will you be home?* No matter how busy she was, she always made time for us during her working hours and at home, blending her roles as a dedicated employee and an ever-present mom with a kind of grace I didn't fully appreciate until later in life.

Looking back, I realize just how much she did for me. And I can never thank her enough. Family was always her priority. She worked tirelessly to raise us with love, instill strong morals and values, and model kindness. She was endlessly creative, always finding unique ways to help us develop our individuality while keeping us busy, happy, and thriving. The countless hours she spent driving us to practices, watching every game, and cheering with all her heart were more than just part of her routine; they were acts of pure love. She made sure we were always on the right teams, surrounded by good people, and learning to work hard and do our best.

As I watched her navigate the constant pull between family, work, and trying to find herself, I witnessed her wrestle with a balance that never quite seemed fair. Without realizing it, she taught me one of the most powerful lessons of my life: I am more than a caretaker, more than a wife or a mother—I have a purpose all my own, a purpose worth fighting for.

I saw what it looked like to give so much that you start to disappear. And I knew I never wanted to lose myself in someone else's version of who I should be.

Now, as a mother myself, I look back and marvel at how much she did for us. You can't fully grasp the depth of a parent's sacrifice until you experience it yourself. That realization has filled me with gratitude, understanding, and empathy for her journey. I'm forever thankful that she taught me how to be a great mother, how to be kind, how to care for others, and how to keep trying through hardship and confusion. She has stood by me through everything, even when we didn't always see eye to eye. Her love has been the steady foundation of my life, and for that, I'll always be grateful.

My Dad

My dad, also from a small town, is a strong, masculine man with an incredibly soft heart. He didn't have the best example of what a healthy father should be, yet he created a loving and healthy home for us. He worked hard to be a father who provided not just for us physically but with love, presence, stability, and dedication to his family.

Just get 'er done!—a catchphrase we grew up hearing again and again. He's hardworking and is usually either bursting with chaotic, fun energy or resting his eyes while relaxing and watching golf on the couch. He was also an incredible athlete in his prime.

He was always up for playing games with us, teaching us the value of hard work, and showing up to every sporting event. My dad was truly hands-on, always ready to play basketball in the driveway, toss a football in the yard, or play cards as a family around the kitchen table. He never showed mercy in any game we played, which made a victory against him—whether in golf, cards, or anything competitive—feel like a true accomplishment.

His dedication to us, his family, is something I will forever be grateful for. Beneath his loud, sarcastic exterior lies a man deeply committed to his faith and family, always striving to do what's right, even if he's made a mistake. He's led by example, instilling in us kindness, hard work, a love for animals, and inclusivity. Our home was always a welcoming place, where strangers, neighbors, and friends felt like they belonged.

I'm forever grateful to have a loving, caring, supportive father and someone who never stopped working hard to provide for his family.

Earlier Generation

My parents' stories include fathers who struggled with alcohol addiction. Both of my grandfathers dealt with alcoholism, a challenge that shaped their lives and rippled through generations. Though I don't know all the details of my grandfathers' experiences, I understand the immense pressures they faced, such as the trauma of war, that likely led them to use alcohol as a coping mechanism. It's heartbreaking to think of the pain they carried, and while their struggles profoundly affected their personal lives, I believe they did the best they could with the tools they had. It was an entirely different mindset, and mental health was still very much stigmatized, an aspect of life you absolutely didn't talk about. Their generation handled life challenges very differently than today.

My heart aches most for my grandmothers and my parents, who grew up in the shadow of that addiction. Witnessing its effects firsthand, my parents made a deliberate choice to break that cycle for our family, a decision that I am deeply grateful for, though they couldn't fully protect us kids. They openly discussed the dangers of alcohol and alcoholism with us throughout our childhood, fostering an awareness that played out differently for each of us kids. Mental health was discussed more and more in our home growing up, and we all worked hard to be open about it, especially later in life.

My Siblings

My sister is four years older than me and a wonderful human being. She's passionate, full of light, and fiercely devoted to her faith and family. She can be a little bossy and controlling at times, too, but it is part of her charm!

Growing up with her was a joy, even with the occasional sibling squabbles, like debating whether the cookies were ready to come out of the oven or seeing life through completely different lenses. She often took it upon herself to keep me in line with how she thought life should be lived, which sometimes created a wedge between us.

I was more of the quiet black sheep, always willing to carve my own path, unafraid to push limits or figure things out the hard way. The road less traveled. She, on the other hand, was more straight-laced and responsible to a fault.

To her credit, during this time, I wasn't making wise choices, and I learned life lessons in the hardest way possible, but I was also carrying the weight of unprocessed generational trauma. That kind of pain doesn't always show up in obvious ways. It lives in patterns, reactions, and the quiet ache of trying to belong in a family while also trying to break free from outdated mindsets.

I did just that.

Even with our differences, we shared a beautiful childhood, one filled with laughter, adventures, and family traditions that I'll always be grateful for. Through the years, she's been a steady presence in my life and an unwavering support system for me and my girls. She's included us in her world with open arms, showing up with genuine care. She has nurtured my daughters in ways that only someone with a deep love for family can. Over the years she's made sure my kids felt cherished and cared for, creating a sense of warmth and belonging in their lives. She's helped us carry on meaningful family traditions, like family Halloween parties and Christmas Eve celebrations that our kids will hopefully keep carrying on.

She has a loving husband, three beautiful children, two dogs, and a fulfilling career as a teacher. Her life is a testament to her dedication, faith, and strong values, and I'm grateful I got to grow up with her.

My Younger Brother

My younger brother Tanner was four years younger than me, and from the moment he arrived in this world, he kept us all on our toes. Daring, restless, and full of mischief, Tanner was always up to something, usually something that made us laugh or shake our heads in disbelief.

Where do I even start?

As a baby, he was already full of energy, wiggling, fearless, strong, coordinated, and always one step ahead of the game. A favorite family photo captures Tanner's personality perfectly. Wearing nothing but a diaper, a neon green and black striped shirt, a motorcycle helmet, and my mom's long pearl necklace, he held a tennis racket and grinned like he was born to rule the world—doing *everything* at once and somehow making it look effortlessly cool.

RECLAIM YOURSELF

At only three years old, he figured out how to pop the screen out of his bedroom window and escape. (Yes, a toddler. A sturdy, clever escape artist!) My mom quickly realized she needed to put my sister and me on what she called Tanner Patrol. This wasn't just a job; it was a lifestyle. Our mission? Keep an eye on him or go on a neighborhood scavenger hunt if he disappeared. More often than not, we'd find him somewhere in the neighborhood, living in his own world, unbothered that we were all frantically looking for him.

He had a knack for disappearing and getting into things he shouldn't, and on another night at gymnastics pickup, he did just that. My mom would often bring him with her to either drop me off or pick me up from gymnastics practice, and he wandered into the men's bathroom, stayed in there a little too long (which was never a good sign), and sure enough, we found him with pink wax on his front teeth, noticing teeth marks in the urinal cake. Yes, you read that right. *The urinal cake.* We were left to wonder: Did he think it was candy? Was he just curious about what might happen if he bit something like that? Either way, that was him, outrageously curious, built with a bullet proof immune system, and always testing the limits.

At four, Tanner had a dream that he could ride without training wheels. When he woke up and saw them still attached, he was furious. He was convinced my dad had somehow sabotaged him. After a bit of pleading, my dad finally agreed to take them off. Tanner hopped on and rode off, full of confidence. . .until he tried to go off a curb and crashed spectacularly. He came back covered in scrapes, but he *knew* he could ride without training wheels, and nothing was going to stop him from proving it. He got back on and rode off down the street, never to use his training wheels again.

That was Tanner. Once he made up his mind about something, there was no stopping him. And that fearless determination followed him everywhere.

Over the years he collected his fair share of injuries—stitches, casts, staples, black eyes, burns, bruises, you name it. He once took a baseball pitch straight to the face, swelling his lip to the size of a baseball. Another time, he crashed his bike into a parked car and broke the headlight with his head because he was too busy trying to read the speedometer. And who could forget the kitchen counter injury? Always in motion, he leaped off the counter but didn't notice a knife had caught in his sweatpants and lodged right into his foot when he jumped and landed. This caused a cut, which later got infected, full of oozing puss until it finally healed. From trampoline springs cutting his nostrils to many scooter and wakeboarding accidents, that was just part of his charm. He didn't just live; he *really* lived. Everything was full throttle.

And while his injuries were a constant, so was his passion. He poured that same full-throttle spirit into every sport he played—football, baseball, basketball, you name it.

We all loved cheering him on in sports, whether it was Little League football, high school baseball, or basketball. At six-foot-four and muscular, he was a force on the field: strong, fast, and ridiculously skilled. He could dunk and move like a blur. He left an undeniable impact wherever he went. But for all his fearless, reckless energy, Tanner had a softer side that balanced him out.

He wasn't just a standout athlete; he was a remarkable person. He loved to read, was an honor roll student, knitted wool hats (yes, really), and baked cakes. He was intelligent, thoughtful, down-to-earth, and, above all, incredibly kind. He was the kind of guy who wanted to be everyone's hero. His hugs were legendary, his hands massive, and everyone loved comparing their hands to his (always feeling a bit small but also a little special).

Being around him just made you feel valued and cared for. He had this magical ability to make people feel seen, loved, and accepted, especially those who might have been struggling or felt out of place. I loved him dearly. One of my favorite childhood memories with him is digging in the dirt, looking for worms for hours, and creating a song we called Pretty Wormy, sung to the tune of Pretty Woman. That day was perfect and a core childhood memory with him.

Tanner continued to thrive in life and sports throughout middle school and high school, building countless friendships, unforgettable experiences, and plenty of internet-worthy highlights and headlines.

High school was filled with late-night practices, road trips, and moments that became legendary among friends and teammates. He was the guy everyone wanted on their team and at their party. Whether it was dominating on the field, pulling pranks, or making everyone laugh until they cried, he had an incredible group of friends and teammates who turned every season into a new adventure.

He had the talent and heart for greatness, both on the court and in life. After high school, he went on to play college basketball, which was no surprise to anyone who had watched him play.

My brother brought joy, laughter, and a gentle kind of love into the world, so much that it's hard to believe someone like him could ever doubt their worth. We all knew he was meant for greatness. We saw it. We felt it. And if love alone could have saved him, he would still be here.

I loved my brother dearly and am forever grateful I got to be his sister.

Me

My childhood was a mix of love, adventure, and moments that still make me smile. We didn't have an abundance of material wealth back then, but we had everything we needed and everything that mattered: laughter, family, close friendships, faith, and the strong values my parents worked tirelessly to instill in us.

Life wasn't perfect, but the constant presence of love made it feel like it was.

Growing up, I was surprisingly quiet and often sought solitude in my room, where I could sit with my own energy and thoughts. In those still moments, I felt the deepest connection to myself, to something greater, and to the quiet whispers of my intuition guiding me. I often kept to myself. I was thoughtful, empathetic, deeply intuitive, and cared about others. But I also wasn't afraid to push back, especially when I felt like someone was trying to control me, which is why my sister and I would get in tiffs!

I also have a vivid memory of a standoff with my dad, both of us locked in a battle of wills in a rocking chair. I wouldn't budge until I was good and ready to let go of whatever was bothering me. (Spoiler: I didn't give in easily, even at that age)

Even as a quiet kid, I was strong-willed, daring, and fiercely determined. I worked hard, thrived on challenges, and naturally gravitated toward leadership roles, whether in school, on the field, or anywhere life placed me.

I did well in school without overthinking it; good grades came naturally. Making friends was easy, and somehow, I ended up with connections that stretched across every group and personality type. I loved beating the boys at recess. Whether it was racing, dodgeball, or any kind of competition, I was all in and usually came out on top. Teachers and coaches gravitated toward me, and more often than not, I was the one picked to lead, team captain, group leader, you name it. I didn't try to be the center of things. . .I ended up there.

Sports were the focus during this season in life. I trained as a gymnast for years, spending four hours a day in the gym after a full day of school. Eventually, I traded the bars and beams for cleats and a soccer ball, and soccer became my world. I played on a competitive team with an amazing group of girls, and we pushed each other through long practices and brutal conditioning. I thrived on the grind. Those practices, games, and road trips are wonderful childhood memories, and I'm still in touch with a few of my teammates today.

I was also the kind of girl who had to learn lessons firsthand. I've always learned best through experience, through feeling, through trying, through living it out myself. It wasn't about defiance for the sake of rebellion but about a deep need for independence. I had to know things in my bones before I could fully believe them. So yes, I pushed boundaries. Not because I wanted to stir the pot but because anything that felt like control or misalignment with my inner compass made me restless, agitated, even.

Up until I was fourteen, life made sense. I was confident, steady, strong, and fully connected to who I was and where I was headed. Things felt aligned. I had a deep trust in myself and in the world around me, like I was exactly where I was supposed to be. Then things began to shift.

Slowly, subtle and not so subtle changes crept in like a low fog, settling over what once felt clear and steady. The sense of certainty I had always carried started to fade, replaced with a kind of disorientation I couldn't quite explain. It marked the beginning of something I didn't have the language for yet, an emotional and psychological strain that my younger self wasn't equipped to name or navigate.

What followed wasn't just a new chapter; it was the beginning of a slow descent. A drift into something far more complicated, tangled, and heavy than I could have ever imagined. These aren't the kinds of lessons you learn all at once. They come in gut feelings you ignore. The confusion you brush off. The excuses you make. The whispers from your soul you dismiss until they get too loud to silence.

RECLAIM YOURSELF

And what I didn't realize back then was that I was already standing at the edge of something.

Something that would shape and nearly shatter the next eighteen years of my life.

Chapter 2

Disconnection from Self

At first, it didn't feel like I was disappearing, just changing, adapting. But I was already becoming someone I didn't recognize. I just wasn't aware of what was happening. Every misunderstanding, every moment I ignored my gut, every time I second-guessed myself was another thread unraveling the essence of me.

The unraveling wasn't just emotional; it started to seep into every part of my life. It showed up in my passions, my identity, and the things that once brought me joy. I began to feel disconnected from sports and soccer, a growing sense of unease mixed with a shift in my personal interests.

After years of pushing myself in sports and being a high achiever, I was burnt out. As puberty hit, my mental wellness began to change in ways I didn't fully understand. By eighth grade, I was grappling with symptoms of anxiety and depression, including racing thoughts, negative self-talk, a sense of feeling overwhelmed, noticeable feelings of unease, restlessness, a lack of interest in things I once loved, fatigue, irritability, and a growing sense of discomfort at both school and home.

During this time, mental health wasn't widely discussed, and while my family wasn't completely in the dark, our understanding was limited. Still, my parents did their best to support me. My dad, in particular, made an effort to be more present, spending extra time with me and even offering more hugs, which was a big deal for him. Back then, most masculine men weren't overly affectionate, and expressing emotions that way didn't always come naturally. But in his own way, he showed up, making sure I knew I was loved. My mom took my mental health seriously in the way only a deeply loving and devoted mother could. She scheduled and took me to doctor's appointments, researched solutions, and never stopped checking in on me. She listened, comforted, and supported me in the ups, downs, and normal adolescent moodiness. I tried the usual treatments available at the time—SSRIs, dietary changes, and more open conversations about mental health. While these helped in small ways, I often still felt the weight of mental health challenges and maturing. I was frustrated and unsure of how to cope.

I continued to navigate junior high filled with hormonal changes, social pressures, and a growing desire for independence. I embraced the excitement of forming new friendships, managing academics, playing club soccer, and exploring crushes and romances. Like most teens at this age, it was a lot to take in, but I figured it out as best as I could, just like every young person finding their way. Life was overall going well, and I thought I had it all under control, but it was just the beginning, and I didn't realize then how much was still ahead of me.

And how quickly everything could change.

As my family continued to watch their daughter shift from a fun-loving, hardworking teen to someone more withdrawn and disconnected, their concern grew. Despite their love and best efforts, they were navigating uncharted territory right alongside me. Again and again, my parents reached out with patience and unwavering support, even when I pushed them away, something that created stress and distance in our little family of five.

I know how much they worried, how desperately they wanted to help me find my way back to myself. Deep down, I wanted that, too, but I was caught in a growing storm of confusion.

My parents, being who they are, especially my mom, never let their love waver. No matter how much I resisted, they stayed constant, always finding ways to remind me I wasn't alone. As a teenager craving independence, their presence sometimes felt smothering, but looking back, I see it for what it was: steadfast, unconditional love. Some nights, I'd welcome them into my room to talk, their quiet presence a source of comfort. Other times, I'd retreat into my own world, choosing isolation. But even then, they found ways to reach me, slipping love notes and little treats under my door, surprising me with thoughtful gifts like plushies and trinkets for my collections and making small gestures that reminded me I was loved, no matter what I was going through.

RECLAIM YOURSELF

My brother and sister made sure I felt that love too. My sister included me in her life, finding ways to spend time together. One particularly memorable outing involved a trip to the mall in her car that we named Clunker, where she mistakenly ran a red light because who has time for stop lights when retail therapy is calling? We spent the next few moments in stunned silence, hearts pounding, before bursting into nervous laughter, extra grateful for our lives!

My brother, Tanner, and I had our own ways of bonding, playing outside, digging in the dirt, jumping on the trampoline, battling it out in video games as I watched him beat levels in Super Mario Brothers or Mortal Kombat, or just lounging together watching our favorite shows. It was a big deal when we got to spend time together, considering how busy we always were with sports and friends.

And no matter what, Sundays were sacred to our family. After church, we'd gather around the table, sharing a meal as a family, a simple tradition that kept us connected through it all.

As the months went on, my personality and behavior shifted in ways even I couldn't ignore, even more obvious as I became involved with the boy who would later become my ex-husband.

I'm not sharing this to cast blame. Teenage relationships can be messy, often shaped by everything we don't yet know about life or ourselves. But this connection? It wasn't just another high school relationship. It became a pivotal turn, one that would profoundly alter the entire trajectory of my life in ways I couldn't have begun to understand back then.

I had no idea the weight I was stepping into. No idea how much it would cost me.

From a bird's-eye view, with the clarity that only hindsight can offer, what I once believed was young love would reveal itself as something much more complicated and far more damaging.

Something that would take years to fully name. . . and even longer to heal from.

Through it all, my family's love remained a safety net.

Even when one family member was physically gone.

Chapter 3

Confusion

From the start, it followed the classic storyline: good girl meets bad boy.

HIM

From my perspective, he was high-energy, rebellious, and unruly. The kind of high-energy you'd question. Trouble, chaos and drama followed him around like it was their full-time job, and rules simply didn't apply to him.

Anger issues and concerning behavior showed up early and never really went away. More often than not, they were brushed off. Chalked up to other things.

That's just him. He just has a strong personality. He's just high-strung. Boys will be boys.

He had a look: he played football, wore a backward hat, had a chiseled jawline, blue eyes, perfectly gelled hair, always wore the newest clothes, drove a nice car, and flaunted Dad's money.

You know the type; we all knew one growing up. The guy with flagrant red flags, anger issues, and chaos all wrapped into one. The kind of guy you know you should avoid, but all of the above drags you in.

Beneath all that cocky charisma, quick wit, and smooth talk, deeper issues were unfolding. There were constant clashes with authority figures: his parents, other parents, his stepdad, coaches, teachers, even his older brother. Fistfights and screaming matches weren't rare; they were normal, often escalating until the cops showed up.

Run-ins with the school, disciplinary actions, brushes with law enforcement; they all started stacking up. Yet, no matter how bad it got, the story always got spun. The behavior was excused, downplayed, or twisted into a narrative where he was the victim. It was often someone else's fault, the teacher, the coach, the system, his family. His mother defended him at every turn.

Eventually, he'd be sent to an all-boys reform school, but that came later. This?

This was everything leading up to it.

This was the unraveling.

ME

In no way am I trying to paint a picture that I didn't have my own stuff. I did. But it was nothing overly concerning. All of the teenage issues I mentioned above were normal adolescent development and struggles, but absolutely nothing I'd faced or previously seen modeled prepared me for the chaos and absolute decline of self-worth, self-esteem, and mental health challenges I was stepping into by being involved with him.

I was one of the popular, athletic girls, but I was inclusive, kind, and empathetic, the type who had friends in every group. I gravitated toward the awkward ones, the outcasts, and everyone in between. My friendships spanned across all circles, guys and girls alike, and no one could understand what I saw in him. He was more of an outsider with a reputation for trouble. People warned me.

But my heart? It was wide open, innocent, soft, untouched by the kind of chaos I was about to be immersed in. I was blissfully unaware of boundaries at this age and unfamiliar with toxicity and the level of manipulation I was about to get taken over by.

In the beginning, it was daydreams, love songs, butterflies, curiosity, and thrill. Like I mentioned, I was adventurous and bold by nature, so sneaking out in the middle of the night didn't feel dangerous; it felt thrilling. Late night phone calls that were way too sexual for this age and skipping class felt exciting, like an escape. It gave me something to focus on during an already turbulent time in adolescence. It felt like us against the world—and our parents. Previously I had no real issues with my parents, but disrespect for adults was rubbing off on me, and developed a chip on my shoulder.

What began with excitement, thrill, and newness slowly unraveled, giving way to confusion, isolation, emotional exhaustion, and a heartache that settled into me, even on my happiest days. I couldn't escape it. It was a constant presence.

Coming from a peaceful home, I had no blueprint for chaos like this. My family wasn't perfect—no families are—but we weren't screaming at each other, throwing punches, making dents and holes in walls, or calling the cops. I didn't know what it meant to live in pure chaos until I found myself in this new reality. The relationship started to isolate me and distract me from the things I actually needed to care about—the things I should've been focusing on, like homework, sports, family, and healthy friendships.

His big mood swings became my issue to diffuse. His problems and ongoing family issues became mine to bear and soothe. His concerning personal behavior took over my headspace and nervous system.

I started losing more sight of myself, believing that love meant self-sacrifice.

That being there for someone meant giving up MY life.

I knew how to endlessly give and forgive but not how to protect my peace, heart, and mind. Not because I didn't love myself but because no one had ever taught me what boundaries looked like. And the more I tried to be there and help him, the more I pulled away from the people who loved me most, myself included. Said with teenaged dramatics:

They just don't understand. He needs someone to love him. His life is hard.

I also didn't know what "codependent" meant. I had no language for things like coercive control or gaslighting. Those words weren't part of my world back then. It wasn't until much later that I began to understand how deeply these patterns can run—how codependent behaviors and survival mindsets are often passed down through generations, especially in families touched by addiction. Even when the addiction itself isn't present, the ways of coping, dynamics in relationships, and emotional habits can still echo.

No one had ever modeled coercive control or gaslighting in my life. I didn't recognize it because it wasn't familiar. All of it was new, and I was learning the hard way—through experience, pain, and slowly waking up to what was really happening.

Over time, I began to feel less confident, isolated, more anxious, and completely wrapped up in how he was feeling. His moods shaped my days. His pain felt like it was mine to carry. I thought that kind of intensity was love.

I was also consumed by shame, guilt, and inner turmoil from beginning a physical relationship.

We were on again, off again. I tried to end things with him over and over, but we always found our way back. My parents tried to intervene.

His parents did too. Nothing stuck. I was still being dishonest about being sexually active with my parents, not because I wanted to deceive them but because the thought of discussing it with my mom was unbearable. In our house, sex before marriage wasn't just discouraged; it was loaded with shame, fear, and judgment. It was loud. I wore that shame like a second skin. Silent. Heavy. Isolating.

My grades began slipping even more, and I lost interest in soccer, in my own life.

I ran away once, full of angst and frustration towards my parents and how they were handling things. I got arrested and ended up in juvie for a day. The kids I met there were facing behavioral issues that were very concerning, and they needed to be there. I'm not sure if my parents told them to send me there so I'd knock some sense in me, and parts of it did, but parts didn't phase me. My parents were understandably devastated. My heart was hardening, and I was becoming someone I didn't even recognize.

The pull between us was strong and toxic. We continued to sneak around, getting caught causing more chaos for both us and our families. I started drinking with friends, often binge drinking (again because I wasn't supposed to be). I had to go to the hospital once because I threw up cinnamon flavored alcohol, which my friends thought was blood.

That was an all time low.

My relationship with my parents was the worst it had ever been. They were furious, devastated, and out of ideas.

HIM

The chaos happening within his home, at school, and in his life, separate from mine, had spun completely out of control. Our relationship was a roller coaster, but I had become a safe place, his constant support system. Although I was acting out towards my parents, it didn't mean I wasn't kind, caring, empathic, and supportive towards him, which only made it harder for me to untangle myself.

He needed me.

The police were being called more, incidents at school kept happening, and the court system got involved.

And then he was sent away to an all boys' reform school.

It felt like heartbreak for my fifteen-year-old self, but it was the beginning of a much-needed shift.

Life started to stabilize.

My mind was clearer; I didn't feel as heavy and confused. I refocused on soccer and school. Reconnected with my family. Things weren't perfect, but they were getting better. I felt better. Clarity was coming back, and so was my self-worth, confidence, and drive for life. I spent a few weeks in Colorado with my cousin and enjoyed a trip to Lake Powell. That summer was full of joy, innocence, fun, and adventure. The kind I was actually craving and needing.

And then he came back the summer before 10th grade...

And just like that, we picked up mostly where we left off.

To be fair, some things had changed. He wasn't getting into trouble as often. He had settled down a little, and life around him felt a bit calmer.

And since he'd left over the summer, my life was pretty much back on track. I no longer had a chip on my shoulder, I wasn't as angry and defiant, and the wedge had lessened between my parents and me.

From tenth to eleventh grade, my life wasn't completely falling apart, but I was still stuck in the same cycle of rebellious behavior, unhealthy coping, and the toxic relationship that only intensified everything.

We were still sexually active, which only added another heavy layer of emotional weight and confusion. Despite everything, we kept sneaking around at night. One night, my dad caught him hiding under my bed.

Looking back, my dad should've kicked his ass—but he didn't.

For reasons I didn't fully understand, my dad was always mostly kind to him, even when he didn't deserve it.

We were still drinking with friends, like a lot of high schoolers, but it felt even more rebellious and heavy, given the religious community we were surrounded by. It was frowned upon.

Most teenagers go through some kind of rebellious phase, testing boundaries and experimenting, which is nothing abnormal. Sometimes, I still ditched class, but for the most part, school, soccer, and my life was on track. Still, I could feel something deeper happening.

I was slipping further and further away from the version of myself I used to know, the lighter, freer girl who wasn't weighed down by secrets and unneeded shame.

Shame, guilt, and confusion clung to me more tightly with each passing day, making it harder and harder to recognize the person I was becoming. I definitely wasn't the same girl who used to light up at hard practices. I wasn't the same girl who loved the grind. I showed up, but the fire was gone. I was checked out, angry and disconnected from the things that used to define me. Even my flip throw, the one move that used to set me apart, felt like just another routine. And my effort in almost everything had become half-hearted. I started varsity as a freshman and again my sophomore year, but I was not the same player my junior year.

I was on an emotional rollercoaster, hooked on the highs, devastated by the lows, and unprepared to admit what was really happening. The confusion was constant.

More self-abandonment.

And what I didn't realize at the time was I was already stuck in the cycle of abuse.

The cycle of abuse doesn't announce itself. It disguises itself as love or passion. As loyalty through struggle. Sacrifice for the greater good. A passionate connection. He's just having a hard time. He doesn't always act like this. He'll change.

Honestly, I thought he would change. He had potential. He was intelligent. He could be so kind, sweet, loving, and understanding when he wanted to be. That glimpse of who he *could* be is what kept me there and my young heart hopeful because WE WERE SO YOUNG, and there were important years in development where things could change.

And when things were good?

They were incredible.

There were weeks of fun, laughing hysterically, gifts, enjoying high school, mutual friends, creating nicknames, making CDs with the newest hits and love songs, helping him with errands, driving around with music blasting, stopping at friends' houses, feeling like we ruled the world. It felt special, and it kept me holding on.

But it never lasted. And when things were bad, they were really *bad*.

Rage would follow. His emotional outbursts left me disoriented, in pain, disconnected from myself, or straight numb. He'd hit things near me, slam his fists down hard on his Jeep car console, screaming about who knows what while I tried to understand what he was upset about and how I could calm him down, feeling completely disoriented and emotionally traumatized.

Without warning, the happy moments would shatter, broken by his emotional outbursts, anger, anxiety, and mood swings. He'd lash out over things I hadn't caused or even been involved in. Once, he berated me in front of a group at a party, and a guy from another school stepped in, confronting him and telling him to apologize. He wouldn't. He yelled at that guy, too, and things got heated.

I brushed it off as a misunderstanding. Broke up the fight. And sadly, I defended him. I said it wasn't a big deal, but it really was, and I was shrinking to keep the peace.

I never witnessed or experienced any other guy within our friend group treating girls this way. Just him.

I never forgot that moment, the way it felt to have someone else see what was happening and call it out.

For a split second, I felt seen. I felt safe. Protected.

I didn't fully understand it then, but something inside me clicked: not every guy treats a girl this way. I logically knew that. But I wasn't living that reality—and it was ongoing and mind-altering. The highs were intoxicating; the lows were disorientating.

This powerful dynamic kept me stuck, convincing me that he needed me even more, but in reality, it was slowly stripping away my soul. It was chipping at my self-worth and my mental health. It was dismantling the peaceful life I once lived.

The sad thing is I wasn't ever questioning *him;* I was always questioning *me.* What did I do wrong? What should I have said differently? How could I fix this? And that—*that*—was a red flag in itself.

And this is what I came to know about abuse years later.

It rarely begins with obvious red flags. It's a gradual descent into a cycle of affection, manipulation, and control. At the time, I often told myself that it was just him. He's different. He'll change, He's just so young. He has family issues.

I'd think to myself that his behavior was unique to him, different from what others experienced. But when I began to understand abuse and saw his behavior for what it was, I realized it was textbook. There was nothing unique or different about it. What made him different was the perceived love and genuine concern I had for him.

The abuse was abuse. No excuses, no misunderstandings, nothing but straight forward, undeniable coercive control and abuse.

His entire personality followed the descriptive, linear pattern of abusive partners, and in hindsight, it was extremely predictable but so easy to get caught up in.

Abuse literally changes your brain chemistry, which adds another element when trying to break free.

It hurt for a long while to realize how much mistreatment I tolerated, even at this age. I'd try to explain how it caused me pain, why the behavior was abusive and hurtful, trying to reconnect and come to a resolve, but I was met with more gaslighting and continued abusive behavior.

He'd say I was somehow equally to blame.

RECLAIM YOURSELF

What I needed to do was walk away and never look back.

And I tried. I tried and tried and tried.

Whether it was through gaslighting, love bombing, or the tangled chemistry of a developing brain, one way or another, we always ended up back together.

And then, in October of my junior year, something shifted. A moment. A choice. An afternoon that slipped in quietly, but would change everything.

I never saw it coming. Maybe a part of me should have. Maybe deep down, I already knew.

Either way, it would ripple through everything.

Life as I knew it would never be the same.

Chapter 4

The News That Changed The Course of My Life Forever

My adrenaline was pumping, pounding in my ears, throat, and chest. Not only was there a very real chance I was pregnant, but the pregnancy test sitting in my sweatshirt pocket was stolen, something that felt almost as heavy as the possibility of the result itself.

We pulled into McDonald's after I'd slipped the pregnancy test off the shelf and walked out of the local grocery store. There was no way I was going to stand at the checkout at sixteen, buying a pregnancy test, fully knowing I wasn't even supposed to be having sex in the first place.

We ordered chicken nuggets and fries and found a booth near the bathrooms. While he ate his nuggets like nothing was happening, I slid off to the restroom with the stolen test still burning a hole in my pocket.

RECLAIM YOURSELF

A woman stood at the sink, washing her hands, when I walked in. She had no idea what was about to happen in the stall next to her, no idea I was seconds away from finding out if my life was about to change forever. The first stall was open. I slipped inside, locked the door, and stood there frozen. My heart was pounding so hard I could feel it in my hands.

I heard the water turn off, the crinkle of the paper towel dispenser, the soft shuffle of her shoes on the tile floor, and the door closing behind her as she walked out. My senses were turned all the way up. My silent breath felt loud, shallow, and fast, like I couldn't quite get enough air.

I slowly reached into my sweatshirt pocket, my fingers brushing against the edges of the stolen pregnancy test box. Even the sound of the box sliding out felt incriminating, like the bathroom stall walls knew I wasn't supposed to have it. My hands shook a little as I unwrapped the plastic. I hadn't read the instructions; I didn't need to. I somehow already knew how it worked. I unzipped my pants and sat down on the toilet. I stared at the test, my vision almost blurring from the possible outcome pressing down on me.

I peed on the stick, capped it, and set it back on the dispenser. And then came the longest two minutes of my life. Those two minutes stretched endlessly, like time itself slowed down, forcing me to sit within myself. My pulse pounded in my ears, drowning out everything else.

And yet, somewhere in the middle of all that fear, I felt calm. If I was pregnant, I had no real concept of what that would mean for me. I wasn't entirely scared, at least not in the way I thought I should be. It was like I'd slipped out of my body, watching myself from somewhere just above, detached and weightless. I don't know if I was dissociating or if some strange sense of surrender had washed over me, but for those few moments, I was both the girl in the stall and the girl observing her.

It was oddly peaceful, like my mind knew something my body was already trying to tell me.

The truth is, I hadn't connected the dots. You never think getting pregnant is going to happen to you. I wasn't even supposed to be having sex, and my brain didn't put the two together.

I'd always been a highly intuitive and level headed person, able to sense things before they happened. My body knew before I did. It had been trying to tell me the truth for months, but I'd gotten used to ignoring it and being far disconnected from myself. But the signs and warnings had been there. In the months leading up to me stealing this pregnancy test, there had been moments, quiet and loud from my own intuition, trying to pull me back to myself. Just weeks earlier, I dreamed I was pregnant—along with a girl I'd been hanging out with who had recently transferred to our school and wasn't the greatest of influences. Looking back, that dream wasn't random. It was a loud warning from my guardian angels, intuition, God, the Universe, or whatever you believe in to stop having sex, but by then, I was too disconnected, too numb, too far from trusting my gut.

It's almost comical looking back because I wasn't even experiencing orgasms at this point in my life. WHY was I still having sex?

RECLAIM YOURSELF

It was deeper and much more damaging. Sex was a way to soothe constant ups and downs, a way to somehow feel connected when I felt so disconnected. It was just another piece of the abuse cycle, another way I stayed trapped without fully understanding why. Same with alcohol. It continued to lower my senses allowing him access to my inner world, when I needed to be placing boundaries. I didn't know how to yet. My energy was constantly being drained, my sense of self eroding a little more each time. Losing that inner voice I was born with was one of my greatest losses during this time. And I didn't even know it.

In the previous weeks, I was exhausted all the time, so fatigued I could barely keep my eyes open. I was falling asleep in all my classes. I felt nauseous, throwing up yellow bile in the school bathroom before heading back to class like nothing happened. I cried over things that normally wouldn't phase me, which felt strange because I wasn't the overly emotional type. If anything, I was the girl who held everything in.

Even soccer, the one thing that had always been mine, started to slip away. I lost my starting spot on the varsity team, the same spot I'd fought for and earned as a freshman and sophomore. My performance was suffering, and my coaches noticed. After practice, I'd collapse into bed for hours, too tired to care about much of anything. None of it made sense at the time. I had never been pregnant before. I didn't connect the symptoms to what was happening inside me. My parents thought I was doing drugs, but I'd never tried drugs.

When the two minutes finally passed, I reached for the pregnancy test.

My fingers felt numb as I picked it up, my eyes hesitant to meet the result.

Two blue lines stared back at me.

I stood there, completely still, a strange sense of calm settling over me. The shock didn't hit immediately; the weight of those two lines gently pressed down on me, slowly wrapping around my mind and body. I didn't panic. I wasn't even crying. I just stood there, absorbing it, the reality of what those two lines meant unfolding in quiet waves. It was as if the world held its breath with me, waiting for the next move while I stayed suspended in time, trying to comprehend what had just happened.

I tucked the test, capped and hidden, back into the pocket of my sweatshirt, washed my hands at the sink, and walked out of the bathroom. My ex looked up at me, waiting for something, an answer, a reaction, anything. I simply whispered, "It's positive."

He dropped his chicken nugget, and without another word, we left. I felt strangely detached from the moment, like I was watching it from a distance. Everything after that seemed to blur together.

I don't remember the specifics, just that I showed him the test in the car, and there was no debate, no big discussion. We sat in his car in quiet, shared uncertainty. To be honest, abortion crossed my mind at that moment. The terror of having to tell my parents and face the world felt too overwhelming. The shame and guilt were suffocating. At that time, women's rights weren't as openly discussed, and abortion wasn't as widely accepted. I wasn't eighteen, and the clinic wouldn't have performed the procedure without parental approval anyway.

The drive to keep everything a secret had been the main focus, so the thought of that option quickly faded.

At that time, I didn't fully grasp the reality of being pregnant. The overwhelming feelings of shame and guilt clouded what should have been a time to recognize the blessing of motherhood and the gift of a child. But I'd never been a mother, so I had no concept of that either.

After a while, he drove me home, and I stepped out of the car, still unsure what was coming next or what to do. I can't remember much else from that night. I walked into the house to the familiar sounds of my parents in the other room and quietly went to my room to think. I shut the door behind me and sank into my bed. What else could I do? I couldn't let on that anything was wrong, that I'd just found out I was pregnant. I also couldn't let anyone see the weight of the world I was carrying.

I decided this secret was mine to protect, and a quiet, undeniable strength washed over me, as if motherhood had already begun to take root within me. In hindsight, I see this as a blessing. I could've gone a completely different route, but a gentle yet powerful force within me made it clear I had to face this alone for now, but I could handle it.

The little life growing inside me was mine to carry, and I moved through it with a calm, unwavering purpose. I didn't have all the answers, but instinctively, I was already stepping into the role of a mother, ready to navigate this new reality, even with the uncertainty of the path ahead.

The following weeks were a whirlwind. Everything in my life seemed to spin out of control, yet somehow, I felt a strange sense of peace settling over me. I was a mom. And for the first time, I felt the weight of it. It was different, yes, but undeniably *real*. While my friends were consumed with the usual high school drama, none of it seemed to matter to me anymore. Their concerns about parties, grades, and who was dating who felt so distant and almost irrelevant. I was living in a reality where the world was spinning around me, but I was in my own universe.

As the weeks passed, my early pregnancy symptoms became impossible to ignore. I was perpetually exhausted, nodding off in class, running to the bathroom to throw up, and missing practices. What passion was left for soccer began to fade, and I was losing weight from constant nausea. My friends started to notice, and my secret slowly began to unravel. The more I tried to hide it, the more it became obvious.

I confided in my best friend, and he told one of his friends. Soon, the news spread like wildfire because nothing stays a secret in high school.

Eventually, our parents found out. They called for a dinner where both families would meet, something that had never happened before, and I could feel the anxiety of it in the air. The dinner was charged with emotion, the tension palpable. They asked if we had something to share, and I took a deep breath. I'm pregnant. I'm sorry. The words felt like they had a life of their own. There were tears and heartache but also relief.

That dinner was terrifying, but it lifted a heaviness I hadn't realized I'd been carrying. For the first time, I was able to speak honestly with my mom about sex—without the crushing shame and judgment there'd been before. She had tried to talk to me at times, but those conversations were always extremely uncomfortable, shameful, and never going the way I'm sure she had hoped.

The dinner was to spill the beans that I was pregnant, but there wasn't a conversation about what was happening next. No conversation about placing or keeping. The days and weeks after, I was in the middle of making a monumental personal life decision:

Should I place my baby for adoption or keep it?

Coercive control was still a suffocating presence in my relationship. My ex and his family made it crystal clear that if I didn't want to keep the baby, he would. There would be no discussion, no compromise. There was no room to consider what was truly in the best interest of the child. It wasn't about mutual respect or what was right for the child; it was about his and his family's way or nothing.

A deeply personal decision became something that felt like an expectation, one where I had no voice or autonomy.

I was already losing so many pieces of myself to an abusive relationship, and facing this life-altering decision felt like another part of me was slipping away. My voice, my sense of control over my own life, felt like it was being stripped, leaving me to feel once again disconnected and disoriented from myself. I was trapped in confusing dynamics with no space or clarity to think for myself. Caught between what felt right for me and the pressures from others, it was as if I had no agency in this decision, only expectations.

In hindsight, I realize that while many women face the hurt of a partner walking away, not having a partner who treats you consistently well can sometimes be a blessing. Oftentimes, I've felt that not having to deal with him and his family and raising my child on my own would've been much easier. A different struggle but one with far less emotional damage.

Despite the overwhelming pressure from his side, I made the difficult decision to explore adoption, so I could be at peace with what I was stepping into and ultimately sacrificing to be a great mother.

My daughter deserved the best of me. With my mom's help, I set up an appointment at a family services center. I walked into that meeting with a heavy heart, uncertain and unsure of what to do. The counselor went over my options, showing me profiles of couples looking to adopt, telling me what the process would be like. I sat there, feeling the weight of it all, and by the time I left, I knew in my heart that adoption wasn't the path for me. For the first time in a while, I felt like I was starting to hear myself and intuition again.

Adoption is a beautiful, selfless choice for many, but it wasn't the choice for me. Even with the pressure from my ex and his family's expectations, I knew this was my child, and I would be the one to raise her. The decision was one of the hardest I've ever made, but my faint yet clear intuition told me I would be a great mother. This is what I needed to do, and she was mine.

Despite the challenges and strain on our relationship, my parents remained my unwavering support. Any child would have been blessed to be raised by them, and they did their best during the years of my rebellion. I knew, even when things felt uncertain, that they would be there for me, helping me raise my child with all the love, support, solid morals, and values they could give. At the end of the day, my childhood home was filled with love. They weren't just my parents; they were a steady foundation.

As the weeks passed, my belly began to grow, and I moved into my second trimester. The morning sickness finally eased, and I returned to school. Walking back into high school knowing everyone now knows you're pregnant is interesting. I had two choices. I could've walked around in shame and hid the entire pregnancy, but everybody already knew. I rocked my pregnancy and lived life the best I could. I went to prom pregnant my junior year and eventually found a program designed for teen moms when I started to show more and didn't feel like continuing regular classes.

Despite everything, my soccer friends and teammates threw me baby showers filled with love, kindness, and support. Sitting there, surrounded by girls my age who I had once played with on the field, felt surreal. Their support meant more than words could express.

In the teen mom program, I met girls facing similar challenges, some pregnant, others with newborns or toddlers. I was struck by their circumstances, some as young as fourteen, others barely seventeen and already raising their second child. It was a whirlwind of emotions, and I couldn't shake the feeling that my life had completely changed forever.

Looking back, it was a strange experience. While I was suddenly thrust into a new and overwhelming reality, the father of my child continued on with his life as usual, seemingly untouched by the shift that had taken place. Meanwhile, I had already begun to understand the immense sacrifices women make in motherhood.

The quiet, constant giving of yourself, the loss of freedom, the shift in priorities, and emotional toll—all of it began to unfold in ways I wasn't yet prepared for. But I knew they were coming. As much as my body and heart had shifted in response to becoming a mother, I realized that being a woman and mother meant navigating a world where sacrifices were often made alone.

The weight of those sacrifices started to settle in.

I got married a few months before my daughter was born.

There was definitely pressure to get married since we were having a baby, but ultimately, it was a choice I made too. Looking back, I'm still not sure it was the right decision, but at the time, it felt like what I needed to do. Intuitively, there was a faint knowledge it wouldn't be for a lifetime. Friends and family came to the wedding. I'm sure it felt surreal for everyone involved. At just seventeen, I moved out of my parents' house and stepped into a completely new life.

His parents kindly revamped their basement for us, and I gave birth in July. Looking back, I'm sure my parents were devastated and felt the loss of so much. Coercive control and power dynamics were still at play even towards my parents. It was his family's way or nothing, and they were all very skilled at manipulating things in their favor, especially given their past.

Our families made sacrifices to help us finish school and support our new family, and for that, I will be forever grateful.

The sacrifices I made played a monumental role in changing the trajectory of his and his family's lives. Before our daughter came into the picture, he absolutely wasn't on the best path, especially outside of our relationship. His issues stemmed long before I met him. However, becoming a father gave him and his family a new sense of purpose and focus other than constant turmoil, trouble, and toxic family dysfunction and dynamics.

I can only hope his family recognizes how this experience helped him grow, lifting a tremendous strain off their entire family dynamics. By choosing to keep my baby and commit to being a great mom, I know I brought a blessing not just to my own life but to theirs, and I did it with the most amount of love despite being treated how no person or woman should be treated.

And I am extremely proud.

CAMEE ADAMS

Returning to School After Being Married and Having a Baby

Returning to high school for my senior year as a married teenager and a new mom was like stepping into a completely different world. While my classmates were wrapped up in dances and social dramas, my reality was filled with diaper changes, midnight feedings, and managing a household. Everything had shifted. Motherhood, especially at such a young age, demands sacrifices that no one can truly prepare for. Suddenly, my life revolved around someone else. From the moment my daughter was born, she and my husband became my priority, and I accepted that without hesitation. I chose to completely stop drinking, stepped up, focused solely on creating a healthy family life, reconnected with my faith, fully embraced my new role, and did whatever was necessary.

Different parts of myself faded away, but for a while, I was content, and new, healthier parts were emerging again.

My senior year was a delicate balance of regular classes and a work-release program, all while navigating the joys and challenges of being a wife and a mother. Despite the obstacles, I proudly walked across the stage at graduation, a milestone made all the more meaningful by the new roles I had taken on. My family looks back through memory books, and one book has my pregnancy, a marriage, and high school graduation all in one year.

I can laugh about it now, but it was a lot for one year!

After graduation, while my friends were heading off to college or exploring the world, I stayed home with my daughter, pouring my heart into marriage, motherhood, and building an uncertain but hopeful future. I grew up fast, learning as I went, and embracing this unexpected path with love and determination.

My journey was mine, unfolding in ways that were different from my peers. I was on a unique path.

I didn't know how unique just yet, and soon, more surprising news would come my way.

Through it all, my family stood by me, offering unwavering love and support. They are nothing short of incredible—not perfect but always doing their best, each of them navigating their lives in the process.

They embody love in its purest form, and I am endlessly grateful and blessed to call them my family.

Life Lessons

Growing up in a religious culture, I was taught that sex before marriage was very wrong, a message deeply woven with shame, guilt, and the looming weight of judgment. It wasn't just about me; it was about how my choices reflected on my family too. Even though I had only ever been with one person, the same person I later married, the judgment was relentless, casting a shadow over what should have been a joyful time in my life.

CAMEE ADAMS

There are far worse things in life than welcoming a beautiful baby into the world at seventeen, and when she arrived, much of the guilt and shame I had carried began to melt away, along with the judgement. But the emotional damage had already been done. The weight of other people's opinions and expectations clung to me for years, becoming a burden I wrestled with long after I should have put it down.

It took me half a lifetime to unlearn the mental and emotional patterns of silent shame that had been unfairly placed on my shoulders and finally reclaim my story for what it truly was: the beginning of motherhood, something beautiful and deeply worthy of pride.

Was I making wise choices at the time? No, but it wasn't abnormal teenage development.

I accepted that and turned my entire life around. I learned, in the hardest way possible, why waiting to have sex can actually be a powerful decision, not a punishment but a form of self-respect and protection. Unfortunately, that's not how it was ever modeled or taught to me at that season in life.

When I finally understood this and loved myself enough to let it go, my spirit felt a little lighter—like a weight I hadn't even realized I was carrying had finally been set down.

As I've matured and developed deeper into my own spirituality, I've come to understand that the insistence on waiting until marriage is rooted in recognizing the beauty and sacredness of creating life. Building a family can be one of the most rewarding experiences in the world, but it must be done with the right person. Without that foundation, it can lead to a lifetime of unnecessary hardship. I can advise adolescents and young adults to practice safe sex and embrace the idea that waiting isn't a punishment; it's a protective measure for your heart, your soul, your future, and your future children.

Protect your energy.

Baby Number Two!

Two years later, at nineteen, I welcomed my youngest daughter, stepping even more into my role as a mother of two. Statistically, about one in five teen mothers (roughly twenty percent) have a second child within two years of their first, a pattern I unknowingly became a part of.

Not so surprisingly, being pregnant at both seventeen and nineteen was physically a breeze for me. Aside from a rough patch of morning sickness in the early weeks, my body handled both pregnancies with strength and ease. Once the nausea passed, life largely returned to normal. I stuck to my fitness routines, jogging from my years as an athlete, stretching daily, and lifting weights. I even continued working physically demanding jobs, from mowing lawns to waitressing, determined to provide for my growing family while staying active and strong.

Staying consistent wasn't just about physical health; it was part of who I'd always been, long before I became a mother. Movement helped keep me stay grounded, present, and gave me space to process life in a way nothing else could. It was my anchor in this season of change, and

I clung to it fiercely—for my own identity and the peace and clarity it gave me.

The decision to have another baby wasn't exactly planned, and while it wasn't shocking like the first time, being pregnant with a toddler had its challenges. A lot more caretaking, diapers, feedings, sleepless nights, and keeping up with now two little wiggly bodies. Looking back, having my daughters just two years apart ultimately worked out beautifully. My little family of four was growing, learning, working, and living life the best way we knew how.

Being married alleviated some of the outside pressures and judgment from strangers and family. When I was out and about with them I was often asked if they were my children and understandably so.

But it didn't erase the emotional highs and lows inside the relationship.

It didn't take long for me to realize that the behavioral issues I was previously dealing with had nothing to do with me or us. I was witnessing the ripple effects of a deeply toxic family system, patterns that ran much deeper than I could have understood at the time. I couldn't have known what I was marrying into. I'd only ever seen it from the outside.

At this time it became increasingly clear that it wasn't our relationship that brought stability. My daughters and I were the steady force. We were the ones bringing peace, calmness, and a sense of reason into the chaos of his and his family's world.

RECLAIM YOURSELF

It was where love, kindness, and true stability lived. And neither me nor my girls deserved to be swallowed by the dysfunction that frequently surrounded us. Regular screaming matches, emotional outbursts, manipulation, mind games, and relentless drama were the norm. I had no idea there could be so much drama, drama that never ended. That's just how life was for them.

On the flip side, when things weren't spiraling out of control, life could actually be really good. We were well taken care of in a lot of practical ways. Physical safety, like being acutely aware of food hazards, stairs that weren't to be walked down when holding babies, and other l child safety concerns were always taken seriously, which is ironic considering how little attention was paid to mental, emotional, and spiritual protection.

We were taken on family trips, extravagant Christmases, supportive in-house babysitters, and a lot of people who loved my girls. They were spoiled endlessly from all sides.

There were real moments of joy, celebration, and support, and for that, I will always be grateful.

Life kept moving forward. My girls kept growing and so did the desire to move out into a home of my own.

His family had helped pay for me to go to esthetician school, and I also received a grant. I was a young mom and qualified for one. I was grateful for all of the help, but I couldn't help noticing my family was slowly getting pushed out. I graduated from aesthetics school with a Master Esthetician license, finished most of my general education credits toward an associate degree, and poured everything I had into motherhood.

I worked hard for every step forward, and I gave back whenever and however I could, especially in the way of bringing peace and calmness to ever stressful family dynamics.

For work during this time, we ran a landscaping business. His father owned a home-building company, and we took over mowing all of their properties. I mowed lawns while pregnant and after, and honestly, I was damn good at it. I wasn't just sitting at home; I was working hard in every way I could, trying to build something, even if it didn't always feel like progress.

I laughed about it at the time, and it was an ongoing joke, but it often seemed that while I pushed through the mowing, someone else was glued to the phone. His constant talking was nothing new; it blended into the background like a never-ending hum. I wasn't aware it was possible for someone to talk to their family that much in a week, let alone every single day. I'm not saying it was a bad thing exactly; some people are just born with the gift of gab, but I had no idea it was possible for someone to have that much to say, all the time, seemingly still attached to the umbilical cord.

While I'd finish the mowing, he'd do all the edging and blowing. I'll give him that.

Your girl could mow a lawn like a pro but edging? That was different. If the properties wanted big chunks taken out of the side of the lawn, all they had to do was hand me the edger! I never quite got the hang of it, but I made up for it with hard work and just getting 'er done!

Moving Out

Eventually, a shift inside me happened. The desire to move was put into action.

I hit a point where I knew it was time to move out. That's how life worked for me at this time. I could be relaxed, easygoing, and chill, but when I knew it was time to make a move, I didn't hesitate and made it happen.

I was very grateful for everything everyone had done for me and my family, but I'd also had enough. I'd had enough of living in his family's basement, enough of feeling trapped under their roof, enough of everyone else's expectations, and enough of keeping the peace and tolerating dynamics I didn't want to continually be immersed in.

If it had been up to my ex, we might have stayed there forever, the cord never truly cut, something I would later understand is common in abusive personalities, especially when an unhealthy bond with a mother figure exists, but in my case the bond with his father was even more concerning.

I was witnessing it firsthand, a strange dynamic that only grew more obvious with time.

I pushed for more. I pushed for better. I spoke up about the enmeshed relationships and voiced that something needed to change. Around that time, one of the properties from his father's home-building company became available. We secured a loan and started the process of moving forward, and for that opportunity, I was truly grateful.

However, full autonomy remained out of reach. Since his father still owned the subdivision, there were always invisible ties. It often felt like I couldn't fully create a life for my own little family and an identity separate from theirs, like I was still woven into a web that was impossible to untangle. His parents were divorced, and it flipped flopped between the two. Quite literally never ending.

But at the time, it felt like progress, a step in the right direction. I was genuinely thankful for the support and opportunities we had. I don't share this to sound ungrateful, only to be honest about the reality: sometimes help came with strings attached, strings I didn't fully recognize until I was already caught in them.

The new transition opened the door to fresh opportunities, new jobs, new possibilities, and in many ways, it marked the beginning of the end. We began earning more and building a life that felt a little more independent. But this time, it wasn't his father we were tangled up with. It was his mother. The web had shifted, and I was still caught in it.

My parents had always followed the steady eight to five routine, living modestly, avoiding debt, and building wealth slowly over time. His family, on the other hand, leaned into entrepreneurship and took bigger risks. Neither way was right or wrong; it was just different. It was a new way of life I was learning as I went.

RECLAIM YOURSELF

He took a new job, a sales position, one his mother connected him to through her speaking opportunities, and some of it was a good fit. His obvious passion for talking on the phone finally started paying off. If running his mouth was a sport, he would've gone pro years ago.

I stayed at home with our girls and lived the stay-at-home mom life, something I'll always be deeply grateful for. Those years with my daughters were precious, and I wouldn't trade them for anything. Alongside that gratitude, there was another reality I didn't fully understand back then.

No one had warned me about this side of motherhood and marriage.

While I stayed home raising our children, I also became the wife constantly at someone's beck and call, running his errands, managing the household, handling his personal tasks like ironing, cooking, cleaning, other things he very much could've done but weirdly demanded I do.

Some women might soak that all up with pride, but for me, it started to feel unfair and servant-like. Like I was an assistant or a mother to manage his entire life, but the same energy wasn't returned when I needed help or the same favors.

There was an obvious unfair power imbalance taking place.

His life kept moving forward while mine felt frozen in place, raising children with no personal freedom or growth in sight. It didn't feel healthy, and it certainly didn't feel normal.

In the beginning, I had been content taking care of everything because I genuinely wanted to, both for my daughters and for my husband.

But over time, the double standards and subtle coercive control I had first experienced back in high school began to resurface, bringing with them a familiar sense of unease I couldn't ignore.

He had the freedom to do whatever he pleased, whenever he pleased, but when I wanted the same, like planning a weekend getaway, it wasn't supported. He wouldn't even watch the kids; I would have to rely on my parents or his just to carve out a few hours for myself. I would get to shop, go to the gym, and run errands, just never go out of town. Which was concerning because he was gone every other weekend—and not for work.

Over time, I started to feel less like a partner and more like a servant. He was rarely home. He was golfing, traveling, or out at frequent guys' nights, and when he was home, he was either gaming or talking on the phone.

Sometimes, I'd tag along, but the group of men he surrounded himself with weren't exactly the kind of crowd you'd hope your young husband would be influenced by. Most were very single, chasing women, still partying, and living a lifestyle completely at odds with the future I thought my young family was trying to build.

I stayed open-minded, supportive, and giving, even trying to have fun, but beneath it all, a growing sense of unease settled in.

I continued to make sacrifices, sacrifices no one had warned me about before marriage. I put my personal growth, career development, and financial independence on hold, naively placing my future in someone else's hands.

RECLAIM YOURSELF

What I didn't realize at the time was that giving up the chance to build a financial foundation and develop a career path and skills also meant giving up a certain amount of choice, autonomy, and freedom. Without my own income and acquired work experience, it became much harder to leave or rebuild. It's one of the hidden costs of motherhood and marriage that society rarely talked about at this time and an important reality I hadn't been taught when I first embraced both with an open heart and the best of intentions. Since then, more women are speaking out, and couples are creating more fairness.

As the years went on, our finances grew. We moved again to a home where I got to help design the interior. Opportunities expanded, but so did more shifts in the relationship—shifts that I could feel, even if I didn't yet know exactly what was coming next.

It also became clear that when it came to our finances, I had no real control. No real transparency. I didn't yet have the education or experience to know how to properly run a business or even what I should have been looking for in our finances. Being so deeply entangled with his family's way of doing things meant there was a constant, uneasy current of deals and financial decisions happening around me without my full knowledge.

The money I helped earn or willingly put on hold to stay at home and raise our family never truly felt like it was mine. He was put on a pedestal, someone I should be grateful for, as if I hadn't also been doing my part. As if managing our home, raising our daughters, supporting his ambitions, caretaking, and catering to his every need weren't equal contributions.

They absolutely were.

I was made to feel like he was somehow extraordinary simply because he was making money, as if that alone defined a greater value and worth. On the surface, so much of life looked and, at times, felt good.

There were truly beautiful days, days full of joy, laughter, and love. We took more family vacations, going to the Caribbean and Florida with just our little family this time, making beautiful memories. We lived in a lovely home and drove nice cars. My girls and I got to experience luxuries like frequent shopping trips and treating ourselves. It was so fun, and I was grateful.

My kids were thriving, enrolled in a private charter school, playing soccer, dancing, and cheering. Driving them to and from school, practices, and activities was time I cherished. Watching them grow and shine was one of the greatest joys of my life. There were genuine moments of happiness, connection, and celebration, moments that replay in my mind often.

Those moments as a mom fill your cup and make you love the sacrifices.

Underneath all of that, there was the other truth showing up much more clearly.

I wasn't a teenager anymore. I was smarter, wiser, more educated on abuse, less tolerant, and more aware of the patterns that had been there all along but had always been excused.

RECLAIM YOURSELF

His behavior wasn't just immaturity or a byproduct of a toxic family dynamic or stress; it was a continual personal choice.

We had matured in more than a few ways, moved through so many challenges together, and overcome obstacles with both sides of our family, personally and as a couple, and still, he chose to continue to behave in the same abusive ways.

In normal, healthy circumstances, I knew couples went through hard seasons. All marriages and motherhood had ups and downs. Sacrifices were just part of building a family. That men can sometimes be assholes, controlling, demeaning, and selfish. I stayed stuck between guilt and obligation, wondering if I was a bad mom for sometimes feeling overwhelmed, even drowned by it all.

But this was different. The constant brain fog, confusion, tightness in my throat, depression, and anxiety were growing stronger, a daily reminder that my voice, my needs, were being swallowed and silenced, but I didn't understand that. I didn't understand yet that your body will tell you everything you need to know. I felt more disconnected from myself than ever before, struggling to think clearly, struggling to stay present.

I was becoming noticeably more withdrawn, slipping deeper into depression. Even people around me started asking if I was okay. "Is she depressed?" they'd wonder. And it wouldn't have been surprising; many mothers experience depression. It's not abnormal. Trying to take charge of my mental health like I had in my earlier years, I went to the doctor, got prescribed SSRIs, kept on my fitness routines, and kept pushing forward.

After all, my life wasn't that bad. It was a phrase I was hearing more frequently...

I was losing parts of myself to the same thing as in my teens, and eventually, I wouldn't be able to ignore it. My life was being smothered, taken over, and it happened in a way that was so confusing for a long time that I thought it was me. That something was wrong with me.

The constant confusion was the sign the abusive behavior was secondary, and the cycle was always there. All of it was becoming louder. And eventually, I would have no choice but to face it.

Chapter 5

The Reason for My Divorce Will Always Be Coercive Control and Domestic Violence.

I didn't recognize the woman staring back at me in the mirror. I had become so far disconnected and withdrawn that even my reflection seemed like a stranger.

With what strength and clarity I had at that time, I arrived at my parents' house with my car packed to the brim, two daughters in the backseat, three squeaky hamsters in their cage, and our fluffy, cream-colored Pomeranian perched on the middle console.

My parents welcomed us with open arms, as they had so many times before, offering a safe place that I will forever be grateful for.

For my daughters, this was now the third time we had left. The previous two times, we had moved into a basement apartment closer to their schools. I always chose to separate because mistreatment wasn't changing, and it only kept exactly each time I came back.

I felt better and much more peaceful when we didn't live together, and I didn't have to be around him twenty-four-seven. I tried to figure out what was wrong with *me* (eyes rolling).

I'm sure they wondered what would be different this time? Was this just another round of the same exhausting cycle?

But this time, *I* was different. I wasn't just leaving. I was rebuilding, this time on my own, not caught in anyone's web that could pull me back in. I was creating a life where love, peace, and emotional safety weren't rare moments we clung to but the very foundation we consistently lived in.

Whether my daughters fully understood it then or not, I was teaching them a lesson I hoped would anchor deep inside them: real love never demands you tolerate mistreatment.

Leaving wasn't about breaking apart our family that I had fought endlessly to hold together. I wanted them to know that walking away can be the bravest, most loving thing you do for yourself *and* for the people you love.

RECLAIM YOURSELF

If they ever find themselves in a situation where love asks them to shrink, silence themselves, or accept what breaks their heart and soul, I hope they remember this.

I hope they remember their mother chose to walk away and, in doing so, showed them they have permission to do the same.

They deserve the kind of love that lifts them up, never the kind that wears them down.

There's a big difference between speaking negatively about someone and telling the truth about ongoing, chosen behavior that doesn't make them look good.

It's never sat right with me to trash him, and I've never had any desire to be part of a smear campaign.

Being this raw and upfront, publicly sharing some of the most painful details of my life, has been one of the hardest things I've ever done.

I don't enjoy reliving any of this, and I'm not trying to convince anyone whose side to take.

And my intention has never been revenge. That's never been who I am.

I'm sharing this part of my story to give hope to the countless women whose stories are never told. I hope that by being this open someone else finds the courage to see their own situation clearly, untangle themselves, and walk away the moment the warning signs appear, not the abuse.

Because large parts of my story, sadly, aren't unique. It follows the painfully predictable timeline of domestic violence and coercive control.

And for years, I carried a misplaced sense of empathy and loyalty toward my ex.

I thought my situation was different. It wasn't in most ways.

What made it feel unique was the love and genuine care I thought I had for him.

I saw the difficult parts of his life. I understood the toxic family dynamics. I saw the potential, the good moments, the history, and that's incredibly common for survivors, especially when you share children.

You're conditioned to believe you owe them something.

That you are an equal contributor.

That they wouldn't have treated you that way if you didn't do something to cause it.

You're supposed to be ride-or-die.

Your life isn't that bad.

And in some ways, mine wasn't, especially when a certain tax bracket became involved.

RECLAIM YOURSELF

But emotional and mental abuse doesn't care how nice your house is. Pain and abuse don't disappear because you can afford vacations or drive a luxury car.

What looks good on the outside can still be deeply abusive on the inside. Appearances don't protect you from harm, and they don't tell the whole story.

Abuse doesn't have to be physical to be real. And it doesn't have to happen more than once to be reason enough to leave.

In my case, it wasn't just one incident. It was ongoing. Repetitive. Cyclical. For years. You don't have to wait for more proof, more pain, or more damage.

You don't have to wait to see if he changes.

The pattern is textbook. I promise you that. The red flags are not random. They are signs of what's coming next. And the longer you stay, the harder it becomes to leave.

When you know better, you *must* do better. Have the courage to leave at the first red flag. Not later. Not someday. *Now*. Please don't let it take years. Please choose yourself sooner. You are worth the most genuine kind of love, protection, and peace. And there are men who will treat you that way, even on your worst days.

A False Narrative

A false narrative surrounding my divorce surfaced, one that suggested that I was the issue, that I wasn't well. There's a sliver of truth in that story. Yes, I battled depression at this time, just like countless others trying to juggle motherhood, marriage, and life itself, especially as a young wife and mother barely out of adolescence.

And when my brother made the heartbreaking choice to end his own life, that didn't help. (Thanks for that, Tanner, said with both sarcasm and love.)

This narrative was nothing more than a distraction cleverly crafted from the real truth hiding underneath. The truth everyone, especially those connected to him, continually swept under the rug.

To this day, I have never been treated as poorly as I was during the span of this relationship.

No one had treated me that terribly before and no one since.

And the mental and emotional abuse was the hardest to heal from. The wounds you can't see are the ones that take the longest to repair, and they took far longer than I ever hoped they would.

Struggling

My struggles at this time weren't born from some personal flaw or weakness; they were a direct response to the environment I was living in. I wasn't just struggling with my mental health. I was drowning in a relationship and marriage that slowly eroded my sense of self, piece by piece, until I hardly recognized the woman I once was. My depression and disconnectedness weren't isolated challenges; they were symptoms of living in a reality that made me constantly question my worth, my mental health, my emotional health, and silenced my voice.

My and my children's sense of peace, security, and self-worth were being chipped away, little by little, year after year.

When a mother is being abused, so are her children. It's not separate. Even if the harm isn't happening *to* them directly, they still feel it. The dynamic is always present, and children absorb it quietly, deeply, and often without words.

I didn't disconnect from my body and mind because I was weak; I disconnected because staying numb felt safer than living in the present. Without realizing it, I was protecting myself exactly like I needed to. A husband and father should provide safety and comfort. In my case, he had increasingly become the opposite.

So yes, I was exhausted, physically, emotionally, mentally, spiritually—and understandably so.

Throughout these marital years, my children and I lived in a subtle fear, a quiet undertow, the state of walking on eggshells, never knowing which version of him we'd get that day. Would there be an exciting shopping spree offered, talks about planning an upcoming vacation, maybe going to the country club that weekend to swim or play golf, out to dinner, or making bets with him to try and win cash?

Or would that day consist of demands and demeaning, degrading language towards us? Or at any given moment, would there be a sudden outburst, irrational anger, or emotional and mental abuse thrown at us, harm created for reasons that made no sense and had absolutely nothing to do with us? We might even experience it all in one day.

Some weeks felt like an invisible test, and no matter how hard we tried, we always seemed to fall short. I'd make dinners like he'd asked, but a drink would get spilled, and he'd blow up, using demeaning language for an accident. We'd miss a call or text from him and then get a slew of texts telling us we were incompetent (more harsh words were used), but if he missed our calls or texts it was acceptable. We said no words, swept it under the rug, and excused it because he was the provider or father.

He could disappear for a few hours without a word, but we were expected to account for every moment of our time for the sake of common courtesy. If we didn't respond, give constant updates, or check in, it was considered rude and inconsiderate. We were glued to our phones, constantly on edge, waiting for the next call or text, unable to fully be present in the moment or enjoy time with friends or family. If we managed to have fun without worrying that missed call from him caused instant stress. We'd be met with a barrage of angry texts or an explosive phone call that would ruin the peaceful, joyful time we'd just spent. The double standards were endless, and he felt entitled to behave this way. He saw no problem with treating us like this, and it wasn't changing, only escalating.

RECLAIM YOURSELF

Until you've lived in the fog of coercive control and manipulation, where hope and hopelessness constantly blur into one, it's hard to understand why leaving feels so confusing. There were times when I doubted the reality of what was happening, especially during those moments when life seemed so good, when he was being so kind.

During these good weeks, there would be incredible kindness, care, and understanding, going out of his way to be extremely giving. He'd try to solve my problems. We'd have fun together, go golfing, have competitive ping pong matches, go shopping, and parent our kids. He'd show up in situations and play the hero, help others navigate their challenges, take my dad golfing and give him unique life experiences, and show my sister and her family thoughtful gestures to make them feel special. He'd tell hilarious stories, and everyone would laugh. He provided for our family and was very engaged with supporting our kids' goals. We were living a comfortable lifestyle, and he was energetic, driven, and fun. Everything seemed perfect until it wasn't.

But when the explosions came, it was extremely disorienting and derailing, leaving everyone off-balance, traumatized, hurt, and confused. It was this unpredictable cycle that kept me and my daughters questioning reality and struggling. I would once again find myself questioning, "Is it really that bad? Maybe I should be more grateful, like he keeps saying. Am I being selfish?" His words would linger:

Oh, poor you—your life's so hard.

I'm such a terrible person, right?

I'm always the bad guy.

You're so ungrateful.

You're selfish, lazy, and stupid.

Your life isn't even that bad.

If I'm so terrible, just leave.

You're so inconsiderate.

Or the sarcastic: I'm so bad, aren't I?

And then, of course: Men are just like this. I knew they weren't because I also had non-abusive men around me.

What he meant was that abusive men are like this. Something he'd been shown since his childhood.

This entire time in my life, I was constantly torn between high highs and low lows.

My sense of self continued to shut down. Every time I tried to point out the behavior, whether calmly, emotionally, or even angrily, I was equally the problem because I was reacting to obvious mistreatment. Somehow, I'd end up apologizing, or he'd push it away, and life would carry on how he wanted it to.

His abusive behavior was repeated, ongoing, and ever-present with no end in sight, which ignited a gut-wrenching feeling of powerlessness, heartbreak, and constant hopelessness inside me.

The mind games, manipulation, and refusal to show consistent respect at home were absolutely exhausting. What made it even more exhausting was knowing he *could* control it; he knew exactly how to act when it served him. Around certain people, he was charming, polite, and endlessly accommodating, flipping the switch on and off like clockwork. I watched him do this time and time again. He was extremely charismatic and good at it.

It often still felt like I existed just to serve him. Not as a family but as a personal servant, always running his simple errands, jumping at his constant demands, dropping anything I had to do at that moment—doing things he was more than capable of doing himself. There was always one more thing to grab, one more task to handle, one more excuse why he couldn't do it himself. My daughters got pulled into it too. Watching them get treated like his personal assistants, expected to drop everything to cater to him, still makes my skin crawl.

Whether it was fetching his drink, running upstairs to grab something, running business errands, or handling things he could've easily done on his own, they learned early that his comfort always came first. It wasn't care; it wasn't love. It was an inflated sense of power and control disguised as helping out or respecting dad. But respect was a one-way street, and we were all stuck on the losing end, especially when he felt like he was losing control.

Waking Up

I began receiving what felt like intuitive downloads, sudden insights and realizations about abuse, the cycle of abuse, how it had shown up in my life, and what I had been dismissing or avoiding. I'd have vivid dreams about specific scenarios, and I started paying close attention, waking up in the middle of the night to write them down so I wouldn't forget.

I knew these dreams were trying to show me something important, and this time, I was listening. As a teenager, I had dismissed that very powerful dream, guidance that would've changed my life if I'd listened and taken the correct actions.

I wasn't going to make that mistake again.

This was my intuition speaking loud and clear, and thankfully, I learned my lesson the first time. I began to see my life with a clarity I hadn't felt in years. The fog had lifted, and I see that as another beautiful blessing. I had been cloaked in depression and fog, and it dramatically lifted during the next few months.

I could finally recognize how he was manipulating everything. I saw the patterns, predicted when they were coming, and even started tracking them on a calendar. Sure enough, about every six to eight weeks, a major blow-up would happen. It didn't matter if I did everything right, ran all his errands, made dinner every night, met all his personal needs. There were no real reasons for him to get upset, only overused justifications for the behavior he had already chosen to display.

This didn't look like empowerment yet, and I didn't have the words for what was happening, but I had reached my limit. I wasn't healed, but I had stopped complying. It looked like snapping over small things, refusing to apologize when I usually would, or finally saying no and not backing down. I started calling out the double standards. I stopped apologizing just to smooth things over. I started yelling back, standing up for my kids, and confronting him when he mistreated us. I became more vocal about what was happening in my home, speaking to my family and his. I became less accommodating and stopped feeling like I owed him special treatment. I stopped catering to his every need and desire, especially when he was out of control about non-relevant issues he somehow spun that I was equally part of. I wasn't.

I knew it because I was one step ahead.

It wasn't my job to soothe or mother him, nor was I interested in trying to show extra love and support, especially with how my kids and I were continually getting treated. It was not okay, and there were no justifiable excuses for any of it.

I looked messy, and it was perceived that way. It started to seem like I was the one causing the chaos, like I was an equal participant. But I wasn't.

I had simply stopped soothing it. Stopped managing it. Stopped keeping the peace.

And when I stopped doing that, his behavior escalated even more. This is also what I learned about domestic violence and coercive control. There's a predictable stage after prolonged abuse where the victim starts fighting back.

This was me. I was her now.

When women begin fighting back, abusers escalate or reverse the narrative, painting the survivor as the problem. This is where terms like **mutual abuse** get misused. In reality, a survivor's reaction to being abused is not the same as the initial abuse.

What Happens When She Starts Fighting Back:

This often emerges during or after prolonged exposure to the cycle, typically after repeated trauma, gaslighting, and learned helplessness wear thin.

This stage might include:

- Setting boundaries (even if shaky)

- Verbal pushback or anger

- Gathering evidence, telling a friend, or journaling

- Emotional numbing followed by bursts of rage or grief

- Physical self-defense in some cases

- Planning to leave or imagining life without the abuser

It reflects a shift from coping to resisting, not always externally, but internally. The woman may not yet be able to leave, but she's no longer fully buying into the abuser's control.

Not Changing

No matter what I did, it continued. And the less understanding I became, the more he seized the opportunity to flip the script, masterfully manipulating situations to his advantage. He got really good at twisting the truth, conveniently leaving out what he'd done to provoke my reactions.

I was left feeling unseen, misunderstood, and completely disheartened, especially around people who could clearly sense something wasn't right but chose not to say anything or step in.

He continued to yell, scream, and overreact to trivial things, just as he always had, and it began to escalate. He started slamming his palm on the stair railing, showing aggression, and pointing his finger in my face while yelling inches from me, sometimes shoving me.

He was going on work trips with coworkers and friends, trips that would raise red flags for most wives. I was still being naive, supporting him, encouraging work/life balance, and thinking he deserved a break and some fun. The fun always seemed to be happening in Las Vegas lately. Yet, I was always expected to stay home, even agreed to it.

When I did go on trips, he wouldn't stay home and watch the kids; I'd have to rely on my parents or his to care for them. I wasn't allowed the same freedom and space to be a person outside of the relationship and motherhood, especially the freedom of continuously going to Las Vegas with just my girlfriends.

One specific evening, after he returned from a trip, I had gotten into the bath before him. I didn't know he was planning to use it, too, and when he realized there wasn't enough hot water left, he exploded. He yelled at me, calling me inconsiderate and selfish, then demanded I go to the kitchen and fill pots with hot water from the sink, as if that would somehow solve the problem.

This kind of controlling, irrational behavior had escalated, especially as he gained more power and status at work, started making more money, and began making increasingly poor choices outside of our home.

The power dynamics and the demeaning behavior intensified. I started retreating, emotionally and physically. Eventually, I stopped sleeping in our room. Some nights, I stayed in the spare bedroom upstairs, sometimes downstairs, anywhere that created space because being near him made me feel physically unwell.

Not just from what was happening inside our home but from a deeper gut feeling that something else was going on. I could feel it. He had started dipping his toe into things he shouldn't have been doing, and I had come to recognize that pattern all too well.

Because every time that happened, his behavior at home would escalate too.

And once again it did.

I kept learning about abuse and learned a common behavior pattern: men who refuse to take accountability for their actions often become even crueler. Instead of facing their own guilt or shame, they project it onto you, blaming, punishing, and controlling to avoid responsibility.

And just like in every abusive relationship, if you stay long enough, the abuse escalates into physical abuse. It always does.

Over the next few months, things intensified exactly as the cycle predicted until, eventually, it turned physical.

Physical Abuse

One night, while I was sleeping upstairs, he came up late, already in a mood about something. We genuinely wouldn't know what had set him off. When I wouldn't engage—no matter how hard he tried to bait me into an argument, I still refused to react—he grabbed a heavy metal permanent marker off of the top of a dresser and threw it at me from across the room. It struck me just above my eye, cutting me and causing it to bleed.

If you know anything about physical abuse, you know it rarely starts with an obvious hit or punch. It usually begins with what seems like playful wrestling, poking, pinching, teasing, testing boundaries to see how much you'll tolerate. It seems harmless.

This wasn't the first incident.

Although I was physically strong and tough, I found myself numbing the pain, even as I mentally acknowledged that things were escalating and deeply wrong.

He had already started shoving me. Getting in my face. Taking my car keys. Tackling me to the ground.

There was one instance when he threw me onto the bedroom floor, leaving a massive bruise across my lower back and glutes that lingered for days.

My physical strength, bolstered by my fitness and health routine, gave me a false sense of security. I told myself I was fine.

So I carried on.

This incident was the moment he crossed a line, when there was no more gray area, no more minimizing. All of it felt like an assault rather than teasing and testing boundaries.

There was a much darker undertow. Intention.

I never thought he'd take it here.

Laying there, dazed and confused, with blood trickling down the side of my face, the way abuse so often leaves you, I knew I had to call for help.

Things were spiraling fast, and I needed to document it. I felt very unsafe, unsettled, and I was in shock.

He was well aware he shouldn't have done this. He said he didn't mean for it to hit me. WHY was he throwing something at me in the first place?

He knew he had also crossed a new line too.

RECLAIM YOURSELF

He left the room, telling me not to call 911, but I did anyway. I felt terrible doing it. How twisted is that? This is part of the abuse women have to work through. Nothing about it feels good or right. You feel bad for the treatment and harm he causes you.

When the officers arrived, they took my statement and pictures while speaking with him outside. I peeked out the window and saw him flip the switch, charming them, staying extremely calm, trying to talk his way out of it. Thankfully, those officers saw through it that night. No excuse he offered could undo what he had done, and that gave me hope. He was charged, had to appear in family court, and a no-contact order was put in place.

And like so many times before, the consequences barely seemed to touch him. Before long, he was back home, and life carried on as if nothing had ever happened. The cycle continued, twisting the narrative until the incident was somehow downplayed, reframed, or made to feel like it was partially my fault.

It wasn't.

It never had been. I knew this now after months of journaling, documenting and doing everything right.

A few days after he came back home, I was met with, *My mom told me to get it expunged because it's bad for business.*

I was taken aback. That was the concern, not my kids' safety, not my safety, not the well-being of our family, not taking accountability, not the reality of what had happened but how it might look?

He was most likely told this because his father had a domestic violence charge against his mother, and years after she tried to get a loan, the lenders wouldn't give it to her because she had been involved with him. So I didn't doubt she mentioned it.

Distancing myself became the only way I knew how to cope. It wasn't some calculated, manipulative decision; it was instinct. My body, my mind, my spirit, and my heart were all screaming for space.

That distance became a whole new marital problem, twisted into proof that *I* was the issue. The blame landed squarely on me, that I wasn't fulfilling my marital duties, and once again, I was left trying to fix something I didn't cause or break.

I was betraying myself over and over, just to keep the peace and my family intact.

Let's be honest, who could possibly feel safe, connected, or cared for enough to want to be physically or sexually close with someone who treats them this way? Someone who tears you down, manipulates, gaslights, and turns a home into anything *but* a place of peace, safety and desire? This wasn't a marital problem.

This was my nervous system doing exactly what it was meant to do, protecting me from harm. The real problem was his refusal to take accountability for his ongoing, deliberate, and chosen abusive behavior.

And further down the road my children would experience an aspect of abuse that hadn't happened yet.

Misplaced Empathy

I still held onto the misplaced hope that because we were so young, things could improve, as we didn't technically choose to be married this young. Of course, there were going to be developmental delays, and marriage was going to be challenging, but by now he surely could see how hurtful his behavior was for me and our kids and choose to change. We weren't teens anymore.

After we moved into our second home, I created a website called "My Teenage Pregnancy" where I detailed cycles of abuse and unhealthy relationships. My intention was to help other teens facing pregnancy by sharing the knowledge and information I didn't have at the time. I didn't fully understand how difficult marriage would be or the true challenges of motherhood. I wished I had known everything I would need to navigate those roles. I wanted to give them a voice to choose what was best for them.

After launching my well-intentioned website, I received an anonymous email accusing me of not appreciating that he stayed with me. The email ignored the coercive control I mentioned earlier, implying that I should be more grateful, as if I wasn't deserving of respect or love in the first place.

This type of anonymous behavior wasn't the last I would encounter, and I had a good idea of who it was. I'd also previously received an anonymous book wrapped in brown paper. The book was called *The Proper Care & Feeding of Your Husband.*

I knew exactly who had sent it. I'd seen this playbook before. It was the same woman who had spent years excusing his behavior and cleaning up the messes he orchestrated over and over again. The umbilical cord had never been cut, and the unhealthy enmeshment was fully intact.

The constant interference had been an issue from the very beginning, even in junior high and high school, and it never let up. Instead of encouraging accountability, she enabled him at every turn, making excuses to keep him from the consequences of his actions, combined with a father who embodied toxic, coercive control and abuse.

He said he didn't feel loved anymore.

Once again, I was flabbergasted.

How dare I stop enabling his chaos, staying silent about his ongoing behavior, especially when it didn't make him look good.

How dare I become less interested in sex.

How completely unreasonable, unhealthy, selfish and unloving of me.

(Insert eye roll here).

More Manipulation-Double Standards Continued

He started taking even more work trips to Las Vegas with coworkers and with his dad. Around the same time, he got really into playing poker, not just online but in Vegas. Again I thought I was being a supportive, easygoing wife by encouraging him to pursue a hobby he enjoyed and was good at.

After all, we got married young, and I wanted him to have the chance to still do his thing.

By this point, we weren't mowing lawns anymore, he had a successful sales job, and we were making good money. I say "we" because it was my life too. I had been there every step of the way, helping build what we had from the ground up.

A woman's presence, warmth, kindness, ability to nurture, willingness to stay home, create a home, and raise our kids requires its own kind of work and sacrifice, work that often goes unseen, unappreciated, and unaccounted for.

He had all the freedom in the world. He had space, time, and constant support to do what he wanted when he wanted. Golfing after work, going out of town on weekends, rarely being at home—that was his norm.

And I wasn't asking for much in return. I wasn't asking him to give up his hobbies. I wasn't demanding perfection or over-the-top gestures. All I wanted was for him to consistently treat me and my kids with kindness and respect. That's it.

Part of this was partially being supported with pursuing my fitness goals. He wanted to golf all the time, so I wanted to start training. It seemed fair enough. I found support in these aspirations. This was one aspect of my life he couldn't control.

We mutually agreed I could hire a fantastic personal trainer. I genuinely enjoyed my training sessions and had a great time training hard and pushing myself.

Regrettably, this positive experience got twisted into accusations of an emotional affair. At one point, I even questioned whether I was developing feelings and admitted it, but in hindsight, I wasn't. The trainer was simply kind to me. I enjoyed working out and looked forward to our sessions. The connection was genuine, supportive, and innocent. Like an uplifting client and personal trainer relationship should be.

What felt good was getting treated with that level of consistent respect and kindness he consistently showed. A light was shone in a very dark spot, and I got another glimpse of how I could be treated.

Looking back on that situation, I can only shake my head.

It's a clear example of how my experience was manipulated, how something innocent and positive was twisted into something I was doing wrong. He was projecting what he was already getting involved in. It was something I genuinely enjoyed, and feeling joy in the presence of another man felt wrong.

As you can guess, the "marital issues" became more and more evident, but again, there was no effort on his part to accept accountability, acknowledge, apologize, or change his erratic and disrespectful behavior. It only continued to escalate, and I didn't mind him being gone so much because I didn't feel well when he was home. Soon, I found out why.

RECLAIM YOURSELF

With him being gone so much, I slowly started to feel more present and alive, and my intuition was screaming at me by this point. With all the work, travel, poker and golf, I had asked him two weeks in advance not to golf on a Sunday so we could have lunch together and spend time as a family.

Even if we weren't in a good spot, that didn't mean we weren't still a family. We both loved our kids. When that Sunday came around, he put on his golf clothes, saying he was meeting his dad to play. I reminded him, somewhat innocently, that I had asked him weeks ago not to and wondered why he was still planning to go. By this point, he was so accustomed to doing whatever he wanted that even a simple request to stay home, one I had made weeks earlier, set him off. He didn't have control and knew he was in the wrong, but he wanted to go anyway.

In response, he spit on me and walked out.

In all of the incidents over the years, this was a new level of disrespect. I stood there, unsure what to do, and he walked out the door.

A few more weeks went by, the "marital issues" escalated to a point where he said, "If you don't do something, I'm going to sleep with someone else."

Up until that point, I genuinely believed I was being a supportive, understanding wife, encouraging him with poker, golf, entrepreneurship, and all those countless trips to Las Vegas. And the coworkers he was traveling with were mostly single.

Those trips? They weren't at all what I had thought.

Come to find out, they were going to clubs, strip clubs, partying, and acting like they were completely single and available.

Meanwhile, I was at home holding everything together, raising our daughters, keeping the house afloat, showing up weekend after weekend as a wife and mother.

And while I was doing that, he had already started crossing lines I didn't even know existed. Unbeknownst to me, he was engaging in behavior that went against the shared values and any understanding we'd had about what was acceptable in our marriage.

More double binds.

A double bind is when you're faced with two conflicting demands or expectations, and no matter which one you choose, you lose. It's a situation where meeting one condition means violating the other—leaving you stuck in a loop where any choice causes harm, especially to yourself. Very common in abusive and narcissistic relationships.

When he first mentioned it, I didn't say anything. Then he brought it up again. And again.

Eventually, I just said, "Fine. You do whatever you want."

By that point, I was completely checked out. The relationship had become far past miserable, far past anything healthy, and I genuinely didn't want to be intimate with him anymore.

I assumed he meant hooking up with someone. I'd heard of couples, after being married a long time, allowing a freebie or something like that. It was never something I agreed with, never something I wanted, and it definitely didn't align with the values I thought we shared. But I didn't know what else to do.

I was stuck in an impossible place, a double bind. Caught between tolerating things that never should've happened in a relationship or continuing to betray myself just to keep the peace.

In short, it was a setup, one he had carefully crafted. A way to justify what he was already dipping his toe into while painting me as an equal part of his poor choices.

A reason to justify it. Once again not taking accountability.

What ended up happening was entirely different.

He kept his same schedule, rarely being home. Either working, golfing, or gambling. All of a sudden, new friends started texting him throughout the day and later in the night.

He said it was a poker friend, which is why they were talking so late.

Long story short, it wasn't a poker friend, and how I found out felt like a series of aligned interventions. Synchronicity after synchronicity kept unfolding.

More Unraveling

One night, he was up late talking to someone on the phone in our office. I rushed into the master closet, pressed my ear to the wall that connected to the office, and I heard him say, "Did you see how long it took her to pick it all up?"

My entire body went numb.

I ran into the office, yelling, WHO THE F*** ARE YOU TALKING TO? He went white as a ghost, hung up, and tried to spin an elaborate tale about a waitress they'd met and how she was picking up a spilled order.

I knew he was full of shit.

This was the beginning of me discovering a lot I had been completely clueless about. But I had been feeling that something was off. The poker friend was actually a stripper and VIP hostess in Vegas. What she was picking up that night was not a drink order. It was dollar bills.

I stumbled upon this by typing each letter in his search bar on his laptop until a page popped up. It had a contact for bookings at the club she worked at, and the next day, I booked a flight to Vegas without him knowing, determined to track her down.

I arrived at the nightclub, asked the guy at the front if he knew the hostess, and he gave me her cell phone number. I texted her and waited anxiously.

RECLAIM YOURSELF

From here more truths started to unfold:

1. She didn't know he was married.

2. They'd been talking for weeks, and he'd been flying down often to see her.

3. She asked about a certain friend of his, someone who was also married with a wife and kids.

4. That friend was also coming down to Vegas with a girl he was sleeping with from their work, and they'd all go on double dates together.

Romantic right?

I continued to text her that day trying to piece everything together. She mentioned specific moments, like talking to him at the end of the day after he was at a waterpark. I knew exactly which day she was talking about; it was a family outing with his stepdad's extended family. She also mentioned him golfing, which made sense because that's all he ever seemed to do lately. He had insisted on going golfing the Sunday he spit on me and walked out because he was talking to her on the drive over.

By now, she had started texting him and asking him questions. He knew I had found out. I never ended up meeting her, and I understood why. I have no idea what he was telling her, but I already knew it was a twisted tale. I was never upset with her. She didn't know he was married, and in hindsight, she did me a huge favor.

I promise you, if any woman can take your husband, she did you a favor.

It was a blessing in disguise.

When I flew to Vegas, I brought a girlfriend with me. I had a chance to experience what single life felt like. We got ready, and I felt amazing! We headed out, and for the first time in a long time, I was excited and joyful! I had always wanted to experience going to a club. Until that point, all I had known was a controlling, smothering, toxic relationship, and the life of a mom. The life of a mom is a beautiful thing **and why I did what I did when I got back home.**

That night out felt magically orchestrated, like everything had fallen into place for a break from the hell I was experiencing. It was a gray area, but given everything leading up to it, it felt right with the undeniable ease of it all. It felt like the night was just for me, and I went with it.

When we walked up to the nightclub, two handsome guys asked us to come in and sit at their table. I was so nervous, but I couldn't help but feel excited. We spent the night with them, dancing, having fun, and enjoying the evening. As the night wore on, one of the guys asked me to go home with him. I felt safe, I was extremely curious and actually wanted to, so I agreed. We didn't have intercourse but a lot of everything else, and more than anything, it was about the freedom I felt, the joy of experiencing something new with someone.

It was romantic, passionate, but not in a toxic way, and for the first time in a long while, I felt seen and cared for. Pleasure.

RECLAIM YOURSELF

Up until that point, I had only been with my ex.

I couldn't stop smiling when I was walking into my hotel. Did that really just happen?

I got back to my room, and when I turned my phone back on, there was a flood of texts. The calls started coming in right after. He was screaming at me, saying demeaning, derogatory things about my body, claiming he was watching me, that he could see me.

None of it was true.

First of all, I was in amazing shape at this time. I knew he wasn't in Vegas nor could he magically see me. He was frantic, he knew I knew what he'd been doing the past few months, and now he was desperately trying to flip the script and instill fear. He wanted to control me, just like he always had. I knew exactly what was happening. I hung up and turned my phone off.

There were no actual feelings for him at this point, but the underlying force of coercive control, fear, having a family, and the ongoing abuse still had a grip on me

It's still mind-boggling to me looking back that he was living an entire double life and had a whole girlfriend on the side, yet he was outrageously upset that I was in Vegas, enjoying my night. It was like he couldn't stand the idea of me possibly experiencing even a fraction of what he'd been doing all these weeks. The double standards continued but even more drastically.

I stayed another day in Vegas, unsure of what to do next. My fight-or-flight response was in overdrive, and I was overwhelmed, still in shock from the chaos of the past forty-eight hours. But surprisingly, I felt a sense of peace and joy. I had genuinely enjoyed the night, experiencing a taste of freedom and being a person outside of being just a wife and mother.

It was freedom that had been suffocated by abuse, double standards, and control for more years than not at that point. I knew the way I was being treated at home wasn't normal, but the desire to keep a family together is real, instinctual, and understandable.

I rarely revisit this week, and writing about it now has stirred up so many emotions. At the same time, it's helped me see just how protected and loved I truly was, how I was being watched over and gently guided through every step of it. Even though I was stepping into a gray area on that trip, it felt right. For the first time in a long time, I was experiencing life on my own terms. I felt genuine happiness, freedom, and joy, and a tiny flicker in me started to rebuild trust in myself.

For years, I'd been carrying so much shame and guilt for getting pregnant so young. For being the worst version of myself during the span of this relationship. I held onto that far longer than I ever needed to, never pausing to give my younger self the compassion and understanding she deserved for all she had endured. Being shamed, guilted, and controlled, then enduring everything else through the years added a layer of complexity to it all.

I have a new sense of grace for her and me, and my perspective has shifted. I don't condone affairs, and in any other circumstance I wouldn't have done what I did, but I can hold space for the truth: in that gray area, I was meant to experience what I did. It was freeing and liberating. It opened my eyes to a world I had forgotten existed, a life where I wasn't buried under fog, pain, confusion, control, and abuse.

It gave me another glimpse of what life could be, and those glimpses would help me break free.

There was so much more to life than what I was enduring.

When I got back home, I was nervous. I had no idea what he was going to do. He didn't know I had gone out, but he knew I was aware of his new relationship and the double dates.

Later that night, we agreed to go to dinner as a family. We chose Olive Garden and sat down. There was a palpable tension in the air, and we didn't talk much. It was more about being with the kids and trying to do something together.

Then, out of nowhere, he asked me if I did anything.

I'm a straight shooter, whether it'll make me look bad or not. I had no reason to hide anything, especially given that he had a girlfriend he'd been flying out to see and sleeping with for months now. I told him I hooked up with someone but didn't have intercourse.

What should've seemed understandable turned into something chaotic and traumatizing in an instant.

CAMEE ADAMS

We had just gotten our soup when, without warning, he reached across the table, flipped the bowl over, and dumped the hot soup onto my lap.

I sat there, my youngest daughter beside me, staring down at the soup spilled on my lap. It was hot, and I tried to stand up, unsure of what to do. People around us started looking, and I felt embarrassed, helpless, and trapped. A waiter came over and handed me a fabric napkin, but I couldn't brush it off quickly enough. I stood up and walked to the bathroom, trying to keep my composure.

When I came out, he was already by the front door, and we all walked to the car in silence. In the trunk, he had a towel, which I wrapped around myself, then sat down. He was seething, his anger spilling over as he started screaming at me in front of the kids. It felt suffocating, hearing him yell while they sat in the backseat.

As we neared our home, he was speeding, threatening to drive me to the Kennecott Copper Mine, which is an older mine miles away, and leave me there. His voice was filled with fury, and he was out of control.

At a stoplight, I couldn't take it anymore. He'd threatened me numerous times, but lately things were escalating. I was strong and in shape, but I was still scared for my safety. I opened the car door, jumped out, and ran down the street in the towel.

I didn't stop running until I saw his car turn left at the intersection, finally disappearing out of sight. My heart was pounding so hard. I was still wrapped in a towel, sprinting down a busier street, but it was late enough that there wasn't much traffic.

RECLAIM YOURSELF

As I made it to the other side of the road, an older pickup truck slowed beside me, and the driver, a man, rolled down his window and asked if I needed a ride.

That's when it hit me—this was my reality. I was a grown woman, running down the street half-dressed, fleeing my husband and home to be approached by another man who I had no idea was safe. I declined the ride.

This wasn't just a bad fight or a moment of tension.

I was living inside the cycle of domestic violence.

And the most sobering part? No one had stepped in.

The signs had been obvious for years, and yet no one truly stepped in; no one forced him to stop. And I get it, at least in part.

Because I kept going back.

The cruel trap of coercive control: It keeps you confused, constantly second-guessing yourself, torn between what's actually happening and the version of reality they've worked so hard to convince you is true. We weren't rebellious teenagers anymore, but I confided in a friend at the time about some of the things that were happening. She was an incredible support system, one of the few people who truly understood the complexity of it all, but she couldn't do anything either.

It had to be me. I told my parents about a few of the recent incidents.

Even his family knew some of it at this point.

But every time I went back, it sent a message, not just to them but to myself. Maybe it wasn't *that* bad. Maybe I *was* part of the problem. If I wasn't walking away for good, then maybe I was somehow responsible for the chaos I was living in.

Maybe they didn't fully understand how bad it really was. Maybe they didn't want to overstep. Whatever the reason, no one did anything.

In that moment, standing on the side of the road with a stranger asking if I needed help, I knew: This wasn't just about escaping him *that night*. This was about taking control of my life and my children's lives, from a situation that was spiraling into something very dangerous.

I couldn't keep waiting for someone to step in.

No one was coming to save me.

I had to save myself, and I truly didn't grasp that until that moment.

It was up to me, and it always had been.

No one wants to intervene in domestic violence; I saw it at Olive Garden when I had just been humiliated. What man dumps soup on the person sitting across from him, especially with two small daughters at the table? It was not normal behavior, and no one had intervened. I understand why. It wasn't their life to get involved in, but someone could've checked on me in the bathroom and asked questions.

No one came.

I had a decision to make.

Jog back home and face a night of hell or keep running down the street and figure out what was next.

I instinctively knew I wouldn't be leaving my kids with him that night, nor would I allow him to manipulate the situation again. At that moment, I had matured in an instant.

It was as if I had put on armor, a newfound strength that prepared me for what I was about to face.

I turned around and began jogging back home, uncertain of what awaited me when I walked through that door. Nerve-wracking silence. I walked upstairs to check on my kids, then to the spare bedroom, where I went to sleep.

Marriage Counseling

The extra relationships weren't what ended it all, but they marked the beginning of the very end. In a strange way, I've always been grateful for all of those women. I never saw my fling again. He remained a pleasant memory, a safe spot I'd escape to when I needed a reminder that there was much better out there than what I was enduring. Even if my lifestyle wasn't as comfortable, the peace and freedom was priceless.

Sadly, I stayed and tried again, beyond my comprehension, to try and fix everything.

I took accountability for what I had said, like a healthy, grown woman—that he could go hook up with someone. But the truth

is, I never should've been put in a position to navigate something like that in the first place.

Heaven forbid he should take responsibility for his own behavior, so I'd actually *want* to have an intimate relationship with him.

I tried to make it right, even when I shouldn't have, because I had a family.

We started marriage counseling, which unfortunately also meant having sex with him again. I even tried to spice things up, wondering if I just wasn't fun enough. After all, he chose a stripper.

The other truth is, it was never about me.

I had always been willing, open, expressive, especially when I was treated with care and respect. She was just easy, available, and part of the atmosphere he was choosing to immerse himself in, surrounded by people who were perfectly fine with his behavior. Men I instinctively knew he shouldn't have been around. And eventually, I learned exactly why.

Through all of this, I was destroying my soul, caught in a painful cycle of self-betrayal that cut deep.

And if I had even the slightest idea of what sexual abuse felt like, maybe this was some small sliver of it. I had to completely disconnect from myself just to get through it.

And I had been working so hard to reclaim my clarity, to rebuild my emotional strength, only to lose myself all over again.

I was doing everything in my power to save something that couldn't and *shouldn't* have been saved.

And then more truths came out.

I still had her number, so I reached out to her to see if they were still talking. Of course, they were. Not only that, but he was still flying out to see her. I had no idea. I was under the impression we were rebuilding trust, that we were both invested in working through this.

A family is a beautiful thing. My kids were worth fighting for, and I was giving it all I had in the most terrible of circumstances.

Meanwhile, he was going to marriage counseling with me and flying out to see her, even on the **same day**. (To say I was shocked is an understatement). The other couple who went through an affair was also going to marriage counseling. The husband genuinely owned up to what he did. He apologized, reestablished trust on **her** terms, and cut off all contact with the other woman. They handled their story completely differently, and that's how I thought working through an affair was supposed to look.

The truth is, couples work through affairs more often than people realize. It's hard, but it's possible, and oftentimes, the relationship is rebuilt even stronger. We wouldn't have been the first to do it.

What made reconciliation impossible wasn't the affairs. It was the ongoing, relentless disrespect, dishonesty, lack of accountability, and continued abusive behavior towards my children and me.

My marriage counselor at the time told me, "Camee, no matter how much whipped cream you put on a cow pie, it's still a cow pie," an epiphany and analogy I found very fitting.

Even when there was this unshakable sense of secrecy, betrayal, and stress, I was still trying to trust him.

I had done everything I could to make the relationship work.

I stopped carrying the misbelief that I was part of the problem.

The real issue was that I kept staying instead of leaving and never looking back.

The line was already crossed.

The line had already been crossed long before I found out about his other choices.

Finding out the relationship was ongoing was excruciating. The betrayal piled on top of everything else, adding a whole new layer to the pain. If you've experienced betrayal, you know what I'm talking about. When something like that is happening behind your back, you feel it deeply. My stomach was constantly in knots. I lived with a perpetual sense of unease, rumination, and anxiety, but I kept trying, thinking it was supposed to be hard.

He was making no effort. He was doing whatever he wanted and was completely out of control. I hadn't agreed to any of it, especially not after we started counseling.

RECLAIM YOURSELF

So, I made the decision to move out again—this time, back in with my parents instead of the basement apartment.

I knew he would try to control the finances, but my parents welcomed me, offered their support, and let me stay. I'm still so incredibly grateful for their love and help.

Yet, the question echoed louder this time: Why didn't he leave the marital home this time, so I could parent our children in stability, especially since he was rarely home and had a girlfriend? Why was I the one always moving out? Also, both of his parents had more than enough resources and space for him.

The answer over the next few months became painfully clear. It was because the priority was never the well-being of our children or what was truly best for them. It was always about maintaining control over me, over them, over money, over assets to maintain the appearance, the double life, and the narrative that I was the issue

I later heard he told people that he kicked me out. Again, I was flabbergasted.

My children and I were afterthoughts. Protecting his double lifestyle came first.

After I moved out and didn't come back like I had in the past, and when he realized he couldn't coercively control me anymore by refusing to pay rent with *our* money, the grand gestures ramped up.

There was love bombing, crying, begging, alongside relentless attempts to contact me.

I refused to engage.

I let him have his time with the kids and never tried to control his relationship with them, even with all the poor decisions he was making. He wasn't physically abusive toward them (*yet*), and as much as I wanted to protect them from the chaos, there was no legal way to stop his rights as a parent because he was living a double life.

I had seen all this before. Just like his career in professional phone talking, he should have pursued acting; his award-winning performances and dramatic personality shifts were astonishing. They could have been convincing to someone unaware of his behavior leading up to these antics. It was truly impressive yet entirely manipulative.

But I wasn't playing the same game anymore.

More Mindset Shifts and Letting Go

Living with my parents was refreshing and I'm sure very stressful for them. With me moving out so young and living with his parents, it was a time in life for us to reconnect, make up for some lost time, and let them spend uninterrupted time with my kids. I was grateful for the help. We were also able to work through some previous challenges that created distance during my adolescent years.

I remember driving past my custom million-dollar home one afternoon, and instead of feeling grief or resentment, I felt something entirely unexpected: peace. Gratitude. A quiet confidence that I didn't need or want that life anymore and maybe never really did. The house, the things, the appearances—they weren't worth what they cost me.

RECLAIM YOURSELF

I wasn't about to keep sacrificing peace just to hold onto something that no longer aligned with who I was becoming.

I knew I was ready to let that house and everything tied to that version of my life go. The image, the material things, the illusion of stability, it just didn't matter anymore. And it never really had.

I wasn't willing to stay entangled in toxicity just to hold on to a title or a house. I had already spent years holding on to things that hurt me, hoping they'd eventually feel safe or meaningful. They never did. My self-worth had already crumbled, and if rock bottom had a basement, I had been living in it.

Letting go wasn't about giving up; it was about choosing peace. Choosing a new story.

I saw how their business operated and how they were living behind closed doors. No matter how shiny or impressive they tried to make it look on the outside, I wanted no part of it. I craved something different. Something real. Something rooted in wholeness and calm.

By the time I found out he had hired an assistant/ nanny who he was also romantically involved with—even before our divorce papers were in motion—I wasn't surprised. She had already moved into my house. But the truth is, I didn't care anymore. I was already gone, mentally, emotionally, and spiritually. Yes, it stung. But I was done.

All I wanted was distance. Space. Clarity. A fresh start to reclaim who I was and rebuild something beautiful with my kids, even if that meant starting completely from scratch.

I got a job working for a nurse practitioner. I kept showing up for my kids. I kept working out. I kept choosing the small things that brought me stability and strength. It wasn't flashy or exciting, but it mattered. And for the first time in a long time, I felt a flicker of relief. A spark of hope.

Those final months had been some of the darkest in my life. I wasn't well, and I knew it. But I also knew that feeling unsafe, confused, and emotionally suffocated was more than enough reason to walk away.

For years, I held onto a narrative that marriage was supposed to be hard—that you stay no matter what. But there's a difference between weathering storms in a relationship and living in a hurricane with no shelter. Abuse isn't a rough patch. It's a soul-level erosion, and no one deserves to live in that.

I was never taught what boundaries looked like. I was conditioned to keep the peace, to forgive endlessly, to hold everything together. But none of that advice applies when abuse is involved. None of that advice keeps you safe.

So I made a different choice.

A brave one. A healing one.

I walked away, not just from a marriage but from an entire belief system that told me my suffering was somehow noble. I broke generational patterns. I dismantled false religious conditioning. I chose freedom over fear. And I am really, truly proud of that.

Being Able to Relax

For the first time in years, I could let myself relax. The constant chaos, uncertainty, inability to plan for the future because I never knew what would happen next, the lack of control over finances, and the overwhelming sense of unsafety had once been my everyday reality. While those things were still very much present, they no longer hovered over me every moment. Alongside that, there was a newfound sense of freedom and hope I didn't know I had.

For the first time in a long time, I believed and hoped that I could move forward and make the changes I had felt so stuck and unable to create for so long.

I'd love to say everything immediately fell into place, but it didn't. Life is life, and it still brought hardship, uncertainty, and challenges, but I had already begun transforming.

I was empowered now, stronger, clearer, and more determined than ever to build a life for myself and my daughters that was defined by peace, hope, and steadiness, not one dictated by control, fear, and manipulation.

More mental clarity came from not responding to continual manipulation tactics, no matter what game or tale he tried to spin that day or week. At this time, my kids didn't have phones yet, and it was near impossible to get any space, but I did my best.

It quickly became clear: if I couldn't be controlled directly, he'd try to do it through the kids—or even through our dog. Eventually, I let him keep the dog full-time. Not because I didn't love her but because she had become just another tactic—another way to keep me tethered.

So once again, I let go. Not out of weakness but out of love. Out of strength. Because the ties had to be severed in every possible way. And that's a kind of strength and resilience you don't know you have until you're forced to find it.

As I continued to stay grounded in my own peace and refused to get pulled into his latest narrative or perceived crisis, more obvious manipulative games started. There was usually some kind of chaos, never ending drama where somehow he was the victim, some urgent disaster that had nothing to do with me or the kids, but somehow, they were expected to get involved and cater to his chaos, and be his support system. I stayed out of it and tried my best to educate my kids on what was actually happening.

He had a way of making my kids feel responsible for his chaos, like we owed him our attention and energy. And if I didn't, he'd flip the script and paint me as heartless, selfish, unforgiving, or cold. I often heard, "She's a bitch." "She's so manly."

If standing up for myself, protecting my kids, and refusing to tolerate whatever he was up to that day made me a bitch and masculine—then yes I was, and I'd do it all again in a heartbeat.

His power over me wasn't real; it existed only because I had unknowingly handed it to him after years of manipulation and emotional wear.

RECLAIM YOURSELF

The attempts to control me never stopped. Whether through finances, material possessions, flashy gestures disguised as opportunities for the kids, or blatant counter-parenting, I could see it all for what it was.

I held my boundaries.

And people, especially those around him, misinterpreted my strength. They thought I was being difficult. Stubborn. Cruel. Playing games. I wasn't.

I was simply standing firm. Enforcing the boundaries I had never had before.

I knew how the script always flipped. And I had zero interest in any relationship, gift, help, or favor dangled in front of me because every time, it turned into a trap. A tool for manipulation.

A weapon to use against me.

And I was done playing that game.

During this time I learned another unseen critical truth: Just because someone is successful in business or financially wealthy doesn't mean they are high-functioning emotionally. It took experiencing platonic and business relationships with other wealthy men, men far wealthier than I'd ever been around, to fully understand this.

Not all wealthy men are abusive. Not all use power imbalances to control their partners, mistreat their ex-spouses, or rely on intimidation. In fact, many of them do the opposite, and it is refreshing to see.

This is also when I realized the behavior wasn't about high stress, building a business, or any of the excuses I used to make for him.

It was simply about who he chose to be. Abusers abuse because they choose to and because it benefits them in some way. Period.

The actions were deliberate and more obvious when I noticed how carefully he chose when and how to behave. Around people he wanted to impress or those he could gain something from, he knew exactly how to act. The abuse happened when no one was watching, or he felt confident no one would believe me.

And all of sudden, he was choosing to be present and making great efforts. It made absolutely no sense. It was ridiculous after everything he was pulling.

And this was the abuse cycle still at play.

He was trying to create the high high to pull me back in.

My Daughters

Healing has a way of peeling back layers you didn't even know were there.

As I moved forward, I began to see things more clearly, especially my earlier years. What I lacked wasn't intelligence or heart—it was boundaries. A deep-rooted sense of self-worth. And the courage to protect that worth, even when it was uncomfortable. I had learned to accommodate others, especially people who treated me poorly, believing that being flexible made me kind. It didn't. It made me small.

I didn't need to shrink for someone else to thrive. I didn't need to put my life on pause, waiting for someone to change or finally get it.

Coming to terms with the truth, that I had been in an abusive relationship for over a decade—was one of the painful realizations of my life. It wasn't something I necessarily wanted to face, but that was the beginning of real healing. Because once I accepted no one was coming to save me, **I began to save myself.**

Some days I felt peaceful and truly ready to move on. Other days, I felt like I was still in the thick of it, trapped in loops of rumination, hypervigilance, and pain that lived quietly in my body. But even in that space, I was learning. Growing. Reclaiming pieces of myself I thought were long gone.

The rumination, especially, was relentless. It was like a quiet hum beneath everything I did, a mental loop I couldn't escape. No matter how much progress I made, it circled back. Analyzing, replaying, questioning. Over and over again.

Healing after abuse is difficult enough. But healing while raising children? While still tethered, legally, emotionally, logistically—to the very person you're trying to break free from? That's a whole different kind of hard.

Still, I stayed committed. I was fighting for a life that felt good on the inside, not just one that looked good on the outside. A life built on peace, not chaos.

And slowly, I started to feel that quiet sense of calm returning. Joy in small things. Laughter with my daughters. Mornings that didn't begin with dread. I was beginning to believe that peace could actually last.

And then, three months later, while living at my parents' house, just as hope was starting to feel real again—the phone rang.

It was 3 a.m.

Chapter 6
3 a.m. Phone Call

For the first time in a long time, it felt like things might finally settle. There was a quiet hope taking root, a sense that peace was on its way. When I moved back in with my parents, things weren't yet moving forward with the divorce process, and mediation was still ahead, but I wanted nothing more than to be done with it.

At the same time, my brother was staying with our aunt and uncle in a small town after spending some time in rehab. The hope was that distance from old habits would give him the space he needed to reset. Working hard on a ranch seemed like the perfect opportunity to build a healthier lifestyle, create new habits, and find a better headspace.

I knew my brother had been struggling more over the past year. That previous Thanksgiving, he came to my house with his sweet, loving girlfriend. Things felt lighter. We laughed and enjoyed the day—it felt like a glimpse of the Tanner we had always known.

We'd all get funny texts from him—pictures of him in Wranglers and a cowboy hat, fully embracing ranch life. I made sure to tell him I loved him and was proud of him, sending encouraging emails and messages. We truly believed he was on the upswing and doing well. . .and then the phone call at 3 a.m. came.

Portable phones were still in at this time, and by some twist of fate, one had ended up in my room that night instead of sitting on its usual charger. It was perched on my dresser when it started ringing around 3 a.m. The shrill tone cut through the silence, but it was the blinking red light that truly woke me—small, flashing, insistent.

I threw off the blankets, my body already reacting before my mind could catch up. I stood up and walked toward the dresser, my heart pounding, my stomach twisting. Late-night calls are never good news. They mean something is terribly wrong. I just didn't know it was going to be about Tanner.

I pressed the talk button and lifted the phone to my ear. Before I could even speak, I heard my uncle's voice—low, heavy, like he was forcing the words out. Then, my dad's voice came through, firm but shaken.

We'll be right there, he said.

And then, in the background, I heard my aunt quietly sobbing.

My dad hung up. I did too.

Panic surged through me as I bolted up two flights of stairs, desperate to reach my parents, to understand what was happening. But as soon as I reached the hallway, I was met by my mother.

RECLAIM YOURSELF

She was hysterical, her body wracked with agony, hands clasped tightly across her chest as if trying to hold herself together. The sound from her was primal, something that didn't just break—it shattered.

"Noooo! Tanner! Tanner!" she screamed, over and over, her voice raw with devastation. I froze. My body went numb.

For the second time in my life, I was both inside the moment and outside of it, watching it unfold from above myself. The air around me grew thick, heavy, suffocating, as if the entire universe had once again shifted.

My senses sharpened, yet my mind felt distant, clouded and razor-sharp all at once. Adrenaline surged through me, my pulse roaring in my ears, but nothing would stop the unraveling of reality around me.

I looked past my mom, searching for my dad. He stepped out of their bedroom, his face pale, his expression hollow. Obviously in shock.

His eyes met mine.

"Tanner's dead," he said.

Two words. Just two.

With those words, time splintered, dividing life into the moment before and the time after our world fractured.

In that moment, instinct took over once again—pure survival mode. My dad didn't hesitate. "**We're leaving now**," he said, his voice firm, resolute. There was no question, no hesitation. "I'm coming with you," I said, my voice steady. I turned and ran downstairs to get dressed, moving through the thick, disorienting reality of what I'd just heard.

The drive to my aunt and uncle's felt like a passage through something unreal, a space where time no longer followed its rules. Five hours blurred together, and then we arrived—stepping into a reality we had never known—one we never could have braced ourselves for. Because how do you prepare for this kind of conversation? When we arrived, they met us at the door, and we hugged. Then, in heavy silence, we stepped inside and sat down, bracing ourselves for the rest of the news.

In their family room, we sat together as they gently walked us through the events of earlier that morning—the hour leading up to the call that had changed everything. We listened as my uncle, a man toughened by years of hard ranch work, had been the one to find Tanner that night. Our hearts ached for him, but we were also grateful—grateful that it was him, someone strong enough to bear the weight of that moment, sparing the rest of us from having to carry it in the same way. My aunt, a nurse who had witnessed years of trauma, was also there—a quiet pillar of strength in the midst of our grief. And for that, we were deeply grateful and still are to this day.

After hearing the details of those final hours—it had only been seven hours before—my aunt and uncle led us down to Tanner's room, the space he had made his own. A quiet reflection of the life he had been trying to piece together. His belongings were neatly put away, his laundry folded, his bathroom organized, his bed carefully made.

And on his bed, he'd left his laptop open and on it were three documents. Three letters.

One for our family.

One for his best friend.

One for his girlfriend at the time.

Looking at his laptop, seeing the documents—knowing they were meant for us—was another moment that felt almost beyond reality. **His final words. His last thoughts.** A part of him reached out, even after he was gone.

There was a deep reverence in that moment, a quiet understanding of what it meant to leave something behind—to make sure we knew his love, to give us something to hold onto when he no longer could. These words weren't just letters; they were pieces of his heart, lovingly left behind for us to remember and a way to ensure that even in his absence, we would feel his presence.

In them, he told us there was nothing we could have done differently. He thanked us, each of us. He made sure we knew, without a doubt, how much he loved us.

And he did. He loved us deeply.

Even when he couldn't find a way to love himself.

Even in his final moments, he was thinking of us. His decision wasn't born out of selfishness but out of a heartbreaking belief that he was somehow sparing us. What he knew about suicide was distorted by the weight of his depression and hopelessness in overcoming alcohol addiction.

His love for us never wavered. Though he made the choice that took him from this world, I often feel deeply grateful that our family received letters. Not everyone gets that, and I can only imagine how much harder the pain of suicide must be without any answers.

We stayed a while longer with my aunt and uncle, wanting to make sure they were okay, not that they would have told us if they weren't. They never let us know how it affected them. Truly beautiful souls. Their grief, like ours, was immeasurable, yet we each carried it in our own quiet way that morning, silent**, heavy, yet deeply understood.**

In moments like that, there are no right words, no clear actions, just the weight of loss and the unspoken bond of those who share it.

Unsure of what else to do, we gathered most of Tanner's things, carefully placing them in the car. Belongings that felt more important than usual, all of it still carried pieces of him we weren't ready to let go of. Then my parents and I left to see him at the funeral home to take the next steps, whatever those were supposed to be. Because what else do you do? It's a strange reality to navigate. Nothing about it felt real, yet there we were, trying to handle it all, a reality we never imagined we'd have to face.

Seeing him one last time. Without a doubt he was still around.

RECLAIM YOURSELF

When we arrived at the funeral home, I felt an urgency to see him. It was not fear, not hesitation, just a deep knowing that I needed to be there with him. There was no question in my mind.

I've always had a quiet fascination with the afterlife. Maybe it was a kind of foreshadowing, a small thread connecting me to this moment long before I knew it would come. Near my parents' house, nestled against the mountains, there was a small cemetery. My friends and I used to wander through it, reading the old headstones, history in the stillness. We found it mysterious, and to me, there was something strangely beautiful about it, something that felt both intriguing and peaceful at the same time.

Back then, I never could have imagined that one day, my brother's name would be etched into one of those headstones—how could I? The thought would have been unthinkable, impossible.

Yet, even then, something about that cemetery called to me. I felt a quiet reverence for that place—a deep sense of love and peace lingering in the mountains and headstones. As if my soul already knew, long before I did, that this place would one day hold something so special to me. A piece of my heart.

Life has a way of preparing us for what we don't yet understand.

When I stepped into the room, my eyes immediately found him. There he was—still yet somehow so present. It had only been about nine hours since he passed. It was impossible to believe he had taken his last breath. He looked so alive, and his presence was filling the space with something unexplainable but undeniable.

He wasn't gone, not yet. I could feel him, his love, his essence, so strong, so real. In that moment, I knew I was experiencing something rare, something special. A moment where love transcended loss, where time stood still once again, and he was still in that room.

He lay on a metal prep table, dressed in a simple hospital gown—the white kind with tiny blue dots tied in the back. It felt like he was just resting, like he might wake up at any second. He looked as though he had just come out of surgery, which, in a way, he had.

The side of his head was slightly swollen, but the wounds had been carefully stitched, barely visible beneath his hair. A faint trace of fluid in his ears was the only heartbreaking reminder of the choice he had made. Yet even that did not take away from the overwhelming presence of love in the room. Instead, it deepened it—a quiet stillness, a sacred reverence, an unshakable tenderness for my brother. In that moment, all I could feel was love—a love so deep, unwavering, and understanding.

I stood beside him, holding his hand, speaking to him softly. I told him how much I loved him, how much he meant to me. And then, in the quiet stillness of that moment, I noticed something so small, so human—his toenails needed trimming, and there was a bit of dirt in the corner of his big toe.

And what else would a big sister do but take care of her little brother one last time?

I found a small tool, gently cleaned away the dirt, lovingly trimmed his nails, making sure he was still looking sharp. I kept talking to him, telling him stories, holding onto the warmth of his hand, refusing to let go of this last moment I had with him. I never wanted to leave.

If I could have stayed in that room forever, wrapped in that energy, in his love, in that peace, I would have.

But eventually, time softly returned, breaking the stillness and I felt a gentle nudge—a quiet knowing that our time for now had come to an end. I leaned down, kissed his cheek, and my parents came in next to have their time with him.

As I stepped out into the funeral home hallway, it felt like I had exited a portal—like I had been pulled from a space back into a world that suddenly felt unbearably heavy. Reality came rushing in. The funeral director had washed the clothes he was found in and gently asked if we wanted to keep them. I took his hat home with me. An LA black on black flat brim fitted hat. I still have it today, a piece of him I can hold onto. I often find myself running my fingers over the bullet hole, the stain—traces of that morning, of the last moments I got to spend with him.

To some, it might seem morbid, but to me, it is meaningful. A tangible reminder of his presence, of how fragile and fleeting life is. And a reminder that the way we choose to live—and love—matters.

Spending time with my brother in the funeral home was one of the most peaceful, sacred, and profoundly surreal experiences of my life. In that space, time didn't just slow—it stood still. I felt like I was floating. The weight of grief and the finality of death softened, dissolving into something divine. I was completely surrounded by his love and presence that filled the room that morning, and I've carried it with me ever since.

The Funeral

A few days later, he arrived in Utah from Nevada, and when I saw him again, he wasn't nearly as alive as he had been when I first held his hand in that quiet funeral home. I knew, in my heart, that those first hours with him were a gift—something I will forever be grateful for.

The funeral and final burial are less vivid. Part of the shock had worn off, and exhaustion was setting in—I remember it all, but what remains the most clear is the memory of dressing him before the funeral as a family. My sister and her husband were there, and for that hour, we stood together—our last time as a complete family here on earth. Saying our last goodbyes.

The line at his funeral and burial stretched endlessly—a sea of people who had loved him, who stood in stunned disbelief. For most, the news was impossible to grasp.

He was the guy who seemed to have everything: a loving family, smart, kind, talent, a bright future. His passing wasn't just heartbreaking; it was shocking.

Friends and family came from every chapter of his life—childhood friends who grew up alongside him, teammates who had played beside him, mentors who had guided him, and family who had loved him unconditionally. So many came who had laughed with him, shared their lives with him and now stood together, honoring the person he was and the impact he had on all of us.

And we are forever grateful to every single person who showed up that day—for him, for us, and for the love that will always surround him.

I don't think Tanner ever truly understood just how deeply he was loved or the impact he had on others. Even now, in his absence, he continues to teach us about life, about gratitude, and about the unseen struggles so many carry in silence.

But that was Tanner. He was so good at making everything seem okay. He would smile, crack jokes, make you laugh, lift you up. He may not have known how to feel good about himself, but he knew, without question, how to make others feel loved. And that's what breaks me the most when I talk about him. He didn't know how to love and feel good about himself. But he never let us doubt how much he loved us.

Tanner's story, like many families, was woven with addiction. Alcoholism was present in both of my grandfathers. Both lived through war and through a time when mental health wasn't acknowledged, let alone talked about. Instead of healing, they coped the only way they knew how. It wasn't just a habit; it was survival.

And whether through nature or nurture, addiction was already in our DNA—waiting, predisposed into our family's history. My parents were aware of its dangers and made sure we were, too, warning us about the risks throughout our childhood.

How that played out for each sibling was different.

My older sister never touched alcohol; it was never part of her life.

I, on the other hand, was curious. I tried alcohol at fourteen, and by sixteen, it no longer had a hold on me, but for a time, it led me down a path that wasn't meant for me. I'm not entirely sure why I drank so young—maybe it was curiosity, maybe it was the need to figure things out for myself. Either way, it was a choice that carried more weight than I realized. Not because I became dependent on it but because I let it into my life without understanding the consequences.

And in doing so, I lost my connection to myself.

It led me to choices I wouldn't have made otherwise, decisions that altered the course of my life.

For Tanner, alcohol was devastating. What may have started as an escape became a chain that pulled him further and further from healing, from himself. Instead of being a release, it became a barrier—a destructive coping mechanism that distanced him from the life he had the power to create. A life that should have been his to shape, free from the weight of addiction.

The understanding of addiction recovery has evolved over the years. At first, the approach was isolation—removing someone from everything that enabled their addiction. Then, a few years later, research shifted, emphasizing connection and support instead of isolation.

When Tanner got out of rehab for the second time, the goal was to keep him away from old habits, old places, and old influences—to give him a fresh start, free from distractions, grounded in hard work. His first stay in rehab had seemed promising; he had gained new coping skills, experienced healing, and formed bonds with a brotherhood that understood his struggles. But the day he walked, he started drinking again.

In the end, neither approach—distance nor connection—seemed to be what he needed. And that is a painful truth to live with.

The thing about addiction is that no matter how deeply you love someone, no matter how hard you try, how closely you follow the latest research, or how many resources you put in front of them—recovery is a choice only they can make.

They have to choose it. Every single day.

And the same is true of suicide. Someone has to choose life, reach for hope, and fight for healing—again and again, day after day. And that is a brutal, heartbreaking reality to sit with.

My brother took his own life five days before his twenty-third birthday.

He was born on Valentine's Day, and he died February 9.

Below is his obituary.

My sister and mom did such a great job writing it, and I reread it often. It makes me teary every time!

CAMEE ADAMS

To the moon

1989 ~ 2012

Tanner Rick Adams, our son, brother, uncle, teammate, and friend passed away February 9, 2012. With loving adoration, we cherish all of our happy memories with him. It was only fitting that the boy who was born on Valentine's Day grew up to be a kid with a humongous heart. Tanner's incredible capacity to love was extended not only to family and friends but also to children, strangers in need, and animals. Tanner was a competitive athlete who never met a sport he didn't like. He was tall, strong, and an intimidating force. Tanner was intelligent, hilarious, witty, insightful, and gave the BEST bear hugs. He loved reading, music, movies, comfy slippers, Duke Basketball, South Carolina golf trips with his dad, A-1 Steak Sauce, and spending time with his family and friends. He loved Natalie, who found a place in his heart that hadn't been touched before. He cherished his four nieces and his nephew, spending countless hours wrestling, teasing, having tea parties, and pillow fights. He filled our home and our lives with laughter, adventure, and a little bit of mischief! Tanner loved and was loved by two amazing sisters who, throughout his life, he leaned on for strength, comfort, joy, and guidance. His parents treasure every minute of every

> day of his journey. We find comfort in knowing we will feel his strong arms wrapped around us again. To the moon! Tanner was born February 14, 1989, in Portland Oregon. He graduated in 2007 from Skyline High School and attended Dixie State, Central Wyoming College, and Univ. of Colo. at Colorado Springs.
>
> In lieu of flowers, please give someone a Tanner-sized hug and be ever mindful of those who struggle.

Losing Tanner changed me in ways I'm still learning to understand. Grief has a way of stripping life down to what's real, what matters most. I wanted more. More peace. More truth. More of the life Tanner deserved but never got the chance to fully live. There was still so much love in my heart, love for my daughters, love for my family, love for the life I had fought to build. And deep inside that love, clarity finally took hold. I knew I couldn't stay where I was. It wasn't about anger, blame, or even survival anymore. It was about choosing something better. For my girls, for myself. For the life we still had ahead of us. And for the first time in a long time, I finally had the courage to say:

Enough.

Chapter 7

Court Proceedings and Being Done for Good

After the funeral, I felt a new level of assurance and certainty that I was done with the relationship. While I had known this before, it was finally time to be finished for good. My brother's passing provided further reassurance and strength to help me keep moving forward.

In the weeks following his death, life felt suspended in time and grief loomed heavily while reality waited to pull me back in. When my ex tried to reach out (*why?*), he was not the person I wanted by my side or the comfort I needed; in fact, he was quite the opposite.

That moment, among many others, was finally the end.

RECLAIM YOURSELF

After everything I had experienced over the past decade, especially the last eighteen months, it might seem unimaginable that anyone would return to a relationship like that. To that, I would say: you've probably never encountered coercive control or true manipulation, two of the biggest reasons why women stay. It's not normal.

It's one of the hardest, cruelest, most twisted, soul-altering experiences, not just while you're in it but in the aftermath. Trying to leave is a battle in itself. And then comes the even harder part: trying to rebuild with the version of you they left behind.

You're the one who's now supposed to go back out into the world and live normally again, let alone thrive, which is also why you see women repeat the pattern. Healing is another full time job, one that doesn't happen in the first forty hours after you finally leave.

I was now stepping into the divorce process, a painful, exhausting battle further burdened by the weight of losing my brother. I was barely holding on, navigating a world that no longer existed, which was disorienting. Life, relentless as ever, refused to slow down.

My parents lovingly loaned me the money (funds were still being controlled, and it's not like I could ask for some) to hire an attorney, which I am sure was stressful for them. They'd just paid for two rehab stays for my brother and then a funeral.

I had originally agreed to mediation, hoping that would suffice. I just wanted out; I didn't want to be tied to any of this old life in any way. However, when I hired a divorce attorney, she uncovered that his initial ownership in the business was listed at thirteen percent. (I didn't even know this).

Almost immediately, they restructured it to reflect just seven percent, cutting my entitlement down to 3.5 percent. On top of that, he quietly sold his shares to fund a new venture, one he still controlled through a trust, without disclosing any of this before mediation.

No surprise they were hiding and rearranging everything, ensuring I wouldn't receive what was justly mine. I had done nothing to deserve unfair treatment in the first place.

During mediation, I insisted on including a clause that entitled me to half of any undisclosed funds or assets. Sure enough, we ended up back in court over funds that had appeared in a joint account that I was supposed to be taken off of after I had agreed to create a separate account for the child support of a mere 403 dollars a month for two children.

Yes, you did read that right: 403 dollars. No alimony, no lump sum.

I didn't take on any of the debt, which they theatrically framed as some grand favor to me, and I also didn't take any part of the business, which was not even brought up.

My attorney had to tell me that.

When I logged into the new account I set up for child support, I was still able to see all the other accounts, unbeknownst to them. I contacted my attorney immediately, and we took the correct steps to contact the judge and go back to court. I was eventually awarded half.

RECLAIM YOURSELF

It was a miracle and a blessing. One that was in the gray area but one hundred percent right given the circumstances.

That money wasn't a windfall or luck; it was the means to provide basic resources that I should have already been entitled to live out of survival mode to raise and care for my kids.

At the time, I was driving Tanner's car after his passing because my own vehicle, the one I had during my marriage, was never in my name and had been taken from me and never replaced. I was living in my parents' basement with my two kids, trying to rebuild a life from nothing, when I had once had so much more.

After I won (they say stole), I was able to pay my attorney, repay my parents, make a tithe to my faith, buy a car, and put a down payment on a townhome, things that were already mine to begin with. I was able to catch my breath for the time being.

Their entire family was furious that I won, that somehow a huge injustice had happened on their behalf. It sparked a wave of anger and more mistreatment toward me from his entire family. Still, I knew, without a doubt, that my victory in court was fair and justified. I had earned every cent by enduring their dynamics, the coercion, and the manipulation that surrounded their son and brother. It was truly mine, and I had earned every cent over the thirteen years.

Looking back, it's disheartening and infuriating how little he was willing to be fair, all while pretending otherwise.

During mediation, the claim was that there was no money. Everything was upside down. There were debts. But if that were true, how was he still living in our million-dollar home? How was he making the payments, driving a luxury car, going on golf trips, rarely in town, gambling, and dating new women? He was definitely not struggling or making sacrifices.

It was even more interesting that his father showed up to mediation, which struck me as odd at the time, especially since my parents weren't there or his mother. We were grown adults, after all. But I later realized he wasn't there to support his son; he was there to make sure I didn't bring up my entitlement to the business because he held the larger share.

They played their parts well. Smiles on their faces. Celebrating that we came to an agreement. Partners in crime. Acting as if everything was fair and settled. But beneath that carefully maintained facade was the silent weight of coercive control that had shaped our relationship since we were fourteen years old.

After mediation, before I found the new funds, he continued to have house cleaners and contractors for lawn work, still taking all the same trips and lifestyle being lived, even unnecessary renovations, without any effort to cut back. None of it made sense. It became clear that mutual support was never the goal. It was about control. About revenge (in life circumstances he single-handedly created), especially after I won in court.

I understood a deeper truth though. I had witnessed and endured the toxic foundation surrounding me: the unethical dealings associated with his father's previous business, the loss of his contractor's license after years in the home building industry, and the rampant infidelity among the men in the new office, including my ex and the two other owners. Dishonesty, manipulation, and coercion thrived among them.

My soul genuinely couldn't remain tethered to any of it. I was not well.

Walking away meant forfeiting what was rightfully mine after thirteen years of building a life together.

We were married for twelve years, and I played a vital role in building our life together, from the earliest days of mowing lawns to being the homemaker and personal assistant, giving up my financial foundation and career growth to raise the children he wanted. These details were often brushed aside. As we achieved success, the lines remained blurred. The ties between him and his parents were never severed, with deals still being made behind closed doors and money moving in ways I was never privy to.

My biggest mistake was not taking control of my finances. I was kept in the dark, trapped and tangled in their never-ending webs of manipulation and confusion. I trusted that fairness would eventually prevail.

I had seen firsthand how things really operated within that family and their businesses, but I didn't fully understand what was actually happening. That's how it always worked. I'd get bits and pieces of information, just enough to feel included but never enough to see the full picture.

And even then, I was never sure if what I was being told was the truth.

And yet, somehow, he continued living the same lavish lifestyle we had always shared while I was left starting over with literally nothing.

If his family had been helping him financially, why wasn't that disclosed? Why was I left to suffer? Surely, some of our money was tied up with them, or, as always, they were making quiet deals. If he could afford to stay in our home, I should have had the same opportunity to raise our children in stability and peace, especially since he was rarely home, doing who knows what. Shuttling the kids back and forth only made their lives more difficult and unstable, yet they did everything possible to make it difficult for me and my kids to start over.

The unfair treatment and power imbalance extended to the custody schedule, which always favored him. He had a nanny/ assistant, two sets of parents, and his freedom while I was the one being punished for his actions. He seamlessly played the victim and then the hero, repeatedly portraying himself as the provider of a better, more favorable lifestyle filled with opportunities and support. In reality, he unfairly created those opportunities at my expense, punishing me for choices he made.

I still don't understand how this happened or why I agreed to it in mediation. The setup required me to work during the week, so why couldn't he manage the kids on the weekends? Yet somehow, the custody arrangement was crafted to ensure he never had weekends.

With his nanny and family support while he traveled for work, I was left with the kids every Thursday through Sunday night, every single weekend. Any attempt to rearrange the schedule was met with a tone suggesting he would take them on weekends. But he was rarely in town. And I was never allowed the freedom to have a life outside of motherhood.

This was all part of the coercive control that persisted even after the relationship ended. I remained entangled in a manipulative dynamic until my kids turned eighteen and the custody schedule began to diminish. It was truly mind-boggling. While I unselfishly and willingly made sacrifices for my kids, it was completely unfair and traumatizing. I was constantly forced into survival mode the entirety of motherhood.

I began to grasp a painful but necessary truth: a man who prioritizes control and power over the emotional well-being of his children is neither a protector nor a provider. If he could leave the mother of his children without resources, fully aware of how it would affect the kids, what did that say about him?

How could it be that I walked away with only 403 dollars a month for two children while he remained in our million-dollar home, drove a luxury car, and built a thriving business that I was absolutely entitled to? I had been there from the start, supporting him and caring for our kids while he built his career, yet he gave me no part of it.

Even years later, when he was building a new home and had to show income, income without his family's involvement, I still didn't take him back to court for more child support. I wanted nothing to do with him. But that decision—made to protect my peace—also allowed the financial and power imbalance to continue.

In the end, I took the loss on the chin and moved forward in the only way I knew how. Some things just aren't worth sacrificing more of yourself over. What I was about to gain, true soul freedom, strength, and the life I was meant to build, was worth every single thing I let burn to the ground.

Chapter 8

Starting to Feel Like Myself Again

A strange stillness was present after everything was over. It wasn't because things were okay, but the kind of calm that comes after a breaking point washed over me—I realized I was still standing, not untouched, not unscarred, but still here. I didn't know exactly who I was anymore. The past few months had stripped so much away. But there was a softness returning. An authentic strength I hadn't felt in years. And even without all the answers, I had one thing that felt brand new: I still felt hope that maybe, just maybe, I was going to be okay. And that was enough to begin again.

That's the thing about healing. It doesn't happen all at once. It begins in small ways. A good day here. A moment of laughter there. A little more energy to fight for the life you deserve.

And that's where I was.

With the financial support for basic resources, we were finally able to move out of my parents' house and into a townhome just a few miles away. I still needed help and support with my kids so I could work, so staying close to my parents made sense.

This move wasn't just about another new address; it felt like my first real *fresh start*. The times before, there was always that lingering question: *Was I going to go back and try to make the marriage work one more time?*

There was no going back. It was finally done.

My parents were truly lifesavers through all of it. In every way that mattered most, they held us up when we needed it.

While I know it was an incredibly stressful time for all of us, part of me believes that having us there, the laughter, chaos, and distraction, helped them navigate their own grief too.

In some quiet, unspoken way, we carried each other through the shock of losing my brother. And I don't believe that was a coincidence.

Once again, life had a way of preparing me for things I didn't even know were coming.

The move itself felt symbolic, like I was physically stepping into the next version of my life. We didn't have much to bring with us, but what we lacked in stuff, we made up for in spirit.

Because that's all I had at this time.

And while I was unpacking, I caught myself smiling. . .

RECLAIM YOURSELF

I was listening to music and putting away my things in the master bathroom when I happened to glance over my shoulder—in the mirror reflecting back at me was a genuine smile.

I paused, turned to face the mirror, and took a long, hard look at myself. I looked tired and worn from everything I had been through, but there was a spark in my eyes, small but unmistakable. And I felt it too. A small spark that was slowly coming back to life.

As we settled in and slowly adjusted to this next chapter, one thing remained complicated. My kids were still being shuffled back and forth. It wasn't ideal, but they were surrounded by love, and everyone did their best to make sure they felt safe, supported, and deeply important.

If there was one thing everyone on both sides could agree on, it was this: loving my kids, even if that love looked different depending on where it came from. Being divorced forced me to let go in ways I hadn't been prepared for. I had to come to terms with the fact that I wouldn't always know what was happening when they weren't with me.

That was hard. Really hard.

Because I did know what happened when I *was* with them. I saw the emotional toll, confusion, and getting silenced without knowing. My greatest fear wasn't just in what I didn't see; it was the manipulation. The quiet erosion of their self-worth and truth. I knew how skilled he and the people around him were at wearing someone down without ever raising their voice, but that happened too. And that's what haunted me most.

It brought on a whole new wave of emotions. I felt unsettled and anxious. It was a different kind of heartbreak I hadn't expected. Up until then, I thought heartbreak looked one specific way, but this was a whole new version, one that came with divorced life.

Turns out, there are plenty of new heartbreaks waiting for you after divorce, and this was just one of them. The hardest part was knowing once again that I didn't have a choice. At least half the month, I had to accept that certain things just wouldn't be in my control, and all I could do was hold onto the hope that the love around them, no matter how different from mine, would serve them in some way. Maybe not in the way I would have chosen, but enough to give them a sense of stability and security in the life we were all learning to adjust to.

I was starting to heal, and that came with confusion.

When you're moving forward, the adjustments that linger in the background are not loud or dramatic but persistent. The kind that reshape your day-to-day life in small, painful ways.

No one warns you about those post-divorce heartbreaks, the ones that creep in quietly when your kids aren't around or when you realize you can't protect them from everything anymore.

And just when you think you've made it through the worst of it, something else rises to the surface.

Grief, and this was a different kind compared to losing my brother.

Doubt.

RECLAIM YOURSELF

That inner voice whispering, *Was it really that bad?*

And that's where the next layer of healing began, not just from the relationship but from everything that came after it. Because surviving abuse isn't always about escaping it. Sometimes, the hardest part is allowing yourself to accept what you experienced was real in the first place.

There's a common experience among abuse survivors that feels a lot like imposter syndrome, this nagging belief that you're not a real survivor, that maybe what you went through wasn't *bad enough* to count. For me, this feeling was constantly reinforced by the phrases continually thrown at me:

Oh, poor you. Your life's so hard.

I'm such a terrible person, right?

I'm always the bad guy.

You're so ungrateful.

You're selfish, lazy, and stupid.

Your life isn't even that bad.

I heard these phrases weekly while I was married and at times after. On the surface, they might not seem overly abusive, but it was the way they were delivered, yelled with confusing authority, sometimes anger, always laced with demeaning intent, and designed to create a power imbalance, especially after already confusing outbursts. Like many toxic and abusive relationships, what made it so hard to leave was the confusion. And that confusion crept back in, even when I was on my own.

Not every day of being married was terrible, and that's what made it so hard to trust myself. There were good times. Whole weeks, even months, where things felt steady. Happy photos, a beautiful home, family vacations, laughter, adventures, and the kind of moments that, from the outside, looked like a good life. And at times, it really did feel that way.

The good times didn't erase the harm; they just made it harder to name. I spent years second-guessing my reality, wondering if I was overreacting, if it really wasn't *that* bad, or if I was just being too critical. That's the thing about emotional abuse; it's quiet, heavy, and disorienting. It sneaks in slowly and convinces you that your instincts can't be trusted. That's a pattern I could see clearly now. I didn't have to slip back into a silent version to keep the peace, which felt nice. It felt like I could just be me, even if this version was still healing.

Rewiring my brain to stop spiraling in self-doubt and emotional confusion became a daily practice. I was actively unlearning the dissonance I had lived in for so long, learning how to stop ruminating, to trust myself again, piece by piece. It wasn't easy. I took two steps forward, one step back and had weeks where I was in the depths of it all again, but I was getting better at finding my way back to clarity and into a version of myself that felt whole and authentic again. I didn't have to keep any secrets, shift into a different version of myself, stay silent, or constantly fight for myself.

RECLAIM YOURSELF

The patterns were clear. The damage was real. It didn't matter if others had been through worse. What I went through left a mark. It wasn't going away just because the relationship ended, and I finally gave myself permission to stop minimizing it.

And more peace came.

The coercive control didn't end when the relationship did. It shifted forms and continued through co-parenting and attempts to manipulate me and my children. There were newfound ways to push buttons and control the narrative, often using my kids to do it. But I'd reached a point where I couldn't keep pushing it down. I had to face it. I had to feel it. And I had to make the decision to stop living like I had no power to change things. Because I did, especially now.

That decision didn't come easily. I had to wake up every day and face the hard emotions, anger, sadness, grief, and resentment. I had to untangle the patterns I'd been stuck in and stop blaming myself for staying. I had made the choice to start therapy, and my therapist reminded me how confusing abuse can be. And when I could see things clearly, I did leave. That shift helped me feel proud instead of ashamed and stuck—like I'd always felt—and helped me keep moving forward.

I started with acknowledging what I'd minimized for so long: the emotional manipulation, the betrayals, the public humiliations, and the constant hypervigilance. I had to stop numbing out, disconnecting from the entire reality of this life, and start *feeling* everything I had buried just to survive. It was extremely overwhelming at first.

But that was the beginning of healing. I got extremely real with myself. I sat with the memories and gave myself grace instead of shoving them aside or letting them disconnect and drain me.

I started to realize my true healing didn't begin until I was willing to *feel* the very painful emotions. And for me, the hardest part was facing just how deeply it affected me.

Admitting that it hurt. That it left me sad, resentful, hurt, numb, victimized, and disconnected.

I kept asking myself, *Why didn't I love myself more? Why did I let someone treat me that way for so many years?* Again, I had to often remind myself how confusing abuse can be.

It's not always obvious. It chips away at you slowly, making you doubt your instincts, your worth, and your reality. When I couldn't turn a blind eye to the truth anymore, I *did* leave.

Instead of feeling defeated, I'd walk out of those sessions feeling proud of myself.

Not because I had it all figured out but because I was finally doing the work to understand myself, admit how painful it all was, heal, and reclaim my sense of self and my God-given personal power.

Healing was not a quick process. There were days I felt isolated, misunderstood, and exhausted. Especially when terms like coercive control or narcissistic abuse weren't widely talked about yet, and I struggled to explain what was happening to people around me and why I was placing new boundaries around my kids and our lives.

RECLAIM YOURSELF

My family and people around me didn't always understand how deeply it affected me, even after the relationship ended. It was done, so I should be fine now, right?

I had to figure out how to help myself, and sometimes, that felt incredibly lonely.

There was grief, too, grief for my brother, for the life I thought I'd have, and for the years lost to survival mode.

The grief for my brother was different though.

There was nothing but love, understanding, and strength while grieving my brother's life.

That process lifted me up, and I felt more love and peace as time went on.

The grief tied to my marriage came with rage, pain, and the deep ache of betrayal, which led to more emotions needing to be processed and healed.

Therapy continually helped me go deeper mentally, emotionally, and even physically. I had to let my body feel what I'd pushed down for years. I'd been carrying so much: memories I tried to forget, public humiliations I brushed off, the deep shame and fear that I thought I had to live with.

I had numbed myself, not with substances or alcohol but by disconnecting completely. I pulled away from life, from myself, from being present in the day-to-day just to get through.

But numbness didn't last forever. Eventually, it wore off.

And when it did, everything I had pushed down came flooding back. And I had to face it. Feel it. Work through it all over again.

This pain became the path. I gave myself grace. I gave myself time. Slowly, I began to rebuild, not just emotionally but as a whole person.

I also realized I couldn't raise my kids to normalize dysfunction or stay silent just because that's what others had done. That wasn't going to be our story.

The way I viewed abuse, what we had been enduring, and what we had accepted had to change.

And that change had to start with me.

Because no one else was going to do anything about it. Even when the behavior was happening right in front of them, people still looked the other way.

I knew I had to be the one to break the cycle, not just for my children but for the women who came before me.

The people that enabled the mistreatment were part of the abuse.

Why didn't they do anything about it?

It will always confuse me. Because it was apparent, especially towards the end.

RECLAIM YOURSELF

As I did the work, something started to shift. The fog began to lift. The deep exhaustion started to ease. Slowly, I began reconnecting with myself, the version of me that wasn't constantly walking on eggshells or pretending everything was fine.

I didn't have to fake the smile or carry anyone's secrets anymore. I was finally reconnecting with myself, the real me. The version that didn't need to pretend everything was fine or shrink to keep the peace.

Healing, for me, became a full-body experience. Emotionally, mentally, physically, spiritually—I had to rebuild all of it.

And the deeper I went, the more I realized: this wasn't just about recovering from abuse.

This was about **reclaiming myself**.

Fitness and The Gym

In a world where so much felt out of my control, movement was the one thing that always brought me back to myself. No matter what was happening around me, whether heartbreak, chaos, or uncertainty, the gym never changed. My yoga didn't judge.

The trails always welcomed me back. It became my ritual, my anchor.

I consider that a blessing.

My motivation and determination toward my fitness goals rarely wavered. It was the one piece of myself that no one could ever take away or control. I had a fierce passion and determination for health, nutrition, and wellness. If there was one thing I could always count on, it was showing up for my workouts, and every day, that grit kept me grounded.

These routines gave me stability, clarity, and a sense of forward momentum. Whether it was strength training, eating clean, walking, hiking, or simply finding quiet on my yoga mat, these practices became my saving grace.

They were more than just habits.

They were how I reclaimed my power.

Later, I began to understand just how connected everything really is. When you're giving your body what it truly needs—good food, movement, time in nature, stretching, breathing—your entire being becomes more capable of processing the heavy stuff. You begin to release stored emotions, and at the same time, you're literally building new cells, creating a whole new internal ecosystem.

Healing for me wasn't just emotional. I was rebuilding from the inside out.

I was becoming a whole new version of myself.

MMA: The Start of BAMF Mode

I didn't go looking for a fight—I just needed a new gym. After moving out of my parents' house, I joined a place closer to where I was living. On the schedule was a class called *Muay Thai*. I had no idea what I was really walking into. Up to that point, my background had been mostly fitness-focused. I'd done fitness competitions, and the closest I'd come to anything remotely like fighting was a college kickboxing class I took for credit. It pushed me, helped me lean out—but this?

This was different.

This was real. Real technique. Real training. Real grit. And I found myself stepping into a world I didn't even know I'd been searching for.

The class was taught by a female fighter, someone I had actually seen fight before. Back then, women's MMA wasn't front and center. It wasn't glamorized or widely recognized. So to watch a woman lead the way, training hard, and teaching the real stuff lit something in me I hadn't felt in a long time.

The classes were small, which meant more one-on-one coaching. I picked things up fast—my body knew what to do. Technique sharpened. Strength returned. My mind cleared. And most importantly, I started to trust myself again. There's something about martial arts. It doesn't just teach you how to fight. It reminds you who you are.

I fell in love with those classes. They pushed me, grounded me, and reminded me how strong I was, so I kept going every chance I could. But pretty soon, I hit a ceiling. I knew if I wanted to go further, I needed to branch out and start learning the full picture: jiu-jitsu, wrestling, everything MMA had to offer.

So, I did what any normal mom would do—I walked into a legit fight gym.

Not a fitness center. A real gym. The kind where most people were training for fights, sparring weekly and chasing pro dreams.

I'll never forget that first day. I walked in nervous, heart racing, completely out of my comfort zone. There were guys who had fought in the UFC. They were legit. This gym was legit, and I suddenly felt like a total outsider.

I was a mom. I wasn't flashy. I wasn't trying to prove anything yet. I just wanted to learn.

I kept showing up. Terrified, awkward, unsure of how I fit in, but showing up anyway. And what I found surprised me.

These men weren't dangerous. They weren't threatening. They were respectful. Gritty and rough around the edges, yes. But kind. Steady. Supportive.

Little by little, they helped me believe I belonged there. They probably didn't realize just how much they were helping me on the mats and far beyond them. They taught me how to fight, but even more than that, they helped me start rebuilding my sense of trust. My confidence. My strength.

Even though I didn't fit the typical mold of a fighter, I was strong. I was athletic. And I was determined to earn my place.

I picked up striking fast. Something about it just clicked. But the ground game? That was different. Something about grappling, about being held down, triggered something I couldn't name at the time. I knew I needed to face it, but the mental block was real.

RECLAIM YOURSELF

Even with the mental block, I kept showing up. Day after day, I trained. Some days I crushed it. Other days, I questioned everything.

There was something empowering about throwing punches and landing kicks with intention. It felt like reclaiming my body one strike at a time, and it made sense to me in a way the ground game didn't.

Wrestling and jiu-jitsu triggered something deeper. It wasn't just physical; it was emotional. I didn't understand it fully at the time, but the hesitation wasn't about technique. It was about healing. My brain did not work as well when it came to logic and logical steps. For so long, it'd been rewired to haywire.

Still, I kept coming back.

And eventually, something shifted.

I started considering the idea of actually taking a fight. Not because I thought I was ready but because I needed to know I could do something that terrified me and survive.

Amateur fights don't come with glory or paychecks. They come with bruises, nerves, risk, and growth. You do it because something inside you is calling for more.

And I answered that call.

Chapter 9

Getting Stronger, Fighting, Fitness

My first fight didn't go as I had hoped, but it turned out to be exactly what I needed. My original opponent dropped out, and a new fighter stepped in. Looking back, I realize I wasn't really ready for the fight; there's a significant difference between training for a match and actually stepping into the cage.

However, I was in great shape and decided to seize the opportunity.

What did I have to lose by trying?

I was tired of feeling stuck in the past, and I knew a new future awaited me, so I took that leap.

I chose a walkout song with a cool intro, even though it didn't hold much meaning for me at the time.

RECLAIM YOURSELF

Typically, a fight walkout song is deeply personal, empowering, igniting! I was still struggling to find that within myself at times, so it made sense that I couldn't find a song that felt that way to me.

Was I really doing this?

Like—me? In a cage? With people watching?

I didn't even know what to do with my face. Should I look mean? Calm? Smiley? Did I just black out during the walkout?

It didn't fully hit me until I stepped into the cage, and by then, there was no turning back.

The announcers introduced us, the bell rang, and just like that—fight mode.

My opponent was scrappy, experienced, and came out strong. She'd clearly been in the cage before. Nothing prepares you for that first adrenaline dump. It's like your whole body tenses up, your brain blanks, and everything you've drilled feels like it's happening underwater.

I was stiff. Hesitant. But I still fought. I landed a few solid jabs and crosses, even threw a couple of clean kicks.

But eventually, she took me to the ground and locked me in a headlock.

It wasn't a perfect choke, but it was tight. I was stuck.

I bit down on my mouthguard, and my breathing was shallow. I kept it as steady as I could and just gutted it out. It was uncomfortable and exhausting—but that's part of fighting.

I made it through the round, and the fight went to a decision, where I lost.

It wasn't the outcome I wanted, but I survived it, and that alone taught me a lot.

I was embarrassed. I hated that people showed up to support me, and I didn't perform the way I had hoped. But in the middle of that disappointment, something clicked. First, just stepping into the cage takes serious courage, and I did that.

Part of being a fighter is accepting the risk of losing and stepping in anyways.

That hit to the ego?

That's what holds most people back. But my ego had already been stripped down. I was a teenage mom. I had lost my brother to suicide. I'd been humiliated in public.

Life had already humbled me in ways the fight world never could.

So while the loss stung, it didn't break me. If anything, it lit a fire.

I finally knew what it was going to take to become a real fighter and what I'd need to do to keep going in the fight game. And despite everything, I still believed I could do it.

RECLAIM YOURSELF

I didn't do half of what I knew in the cage that night.

More importantly, I *wanted* to. I was more than willing to put in the work, and fighting demands a relentless grind.

If there was one thing I knew how to do, it was work.

I walked away from that fight knowing it was time to sharpen my mental game. That night, my mind was filled with doubts that had nothing to do with fighting, and that had to change. If I wanted to grow, I needed to start sparring more and finally commit to the ground work. Physical conditioning alone wasn't going to be enough anymore.

And so, I got to work.

After that first fight, something shifted.

It didn't go the way I had hoped, but I wasn't discouraged. I was determined. I had stepped into the cage once, and that was enough to show me I belonged. I just needed to keep growing.

So I kept showing up at the fight gym.

The ground game still gave me pause. I didn't dive in right away. There was a mental block I couldn't quite name, some kind of fear I hadn't fully unpacked yet. But I didn't let it stop me. I just kept coming back, one session at a time.

Balancing motherhood, work, and fight training wasn't easy—far from it. But I had found something worth holding onto—something that grounded me and gave me purpose outside of all the roles I filled.

So I stayed as consistent as I could.

I stuck to my meal plans. I woke up early. I went to work. I kept a routine that made sense for our life. On parenting days, I'd scoop my girls up from school, get them settled with practice or homework, and once they were good, I'd head to the gym for a ninety-minute session. If they needed anything, they could call me. The fight gym was only fifteen minutes away.

On the days I didn't have them, I trained longer and added in yoga or a lift. I poured myself into the discipline, not just because I believed I could be a great fighter—but because the process was shaping every part of me.

And one of the sweetest parts?

My girls were getting serious about their sports too. They ate clean with me, got excited about our schedules, and understood the rhythm of commitment and consistency. On weekends, we were all in, driving from basketball tournaments to volleyball games, then spending time with family.

We were building something real—together.

It felt like we were all growing together, and that was fun!

Dating wasn't my focus, but every now and then, I put myself out there. There was always this quiet unease around it. Every time I even began to move forward, chaos would follow. My kids would get asked questions about my personal life, and somehow, it always stirred up drama that felt totally unnecessary. It became clear that, for now, it just wasn't worth the disruption.

And let's just say...healing doesn't always come with perfect clarity. I still found myself drawn to the wrong connections and uninterested in the right ones. I knew I wasn't fully ready yet, and that was okay.

There were two kinds of relationships I definitely should've avoided (I'll take full accountability for that), and two truly great men I just wasn't ready for or really wanted to live the stay-at-home lifestyle they wanted. I'd already been married. I wasn't looking to fill a void or play house again. I wanted to fight, grow, heal, and pursue my goals before anything else other than my kids.

Thankfully, I caught it before it was too late. I could feel when something wasn't aligned—and I listened. That alone was growth.

So instead, I poured my energy into training. It was steady. It was honest. It gave back everything I put into it and never asked me to be anything but myself. It became the space where I reconnected with my power—the kind that didn't depend on anyone else.

I was raising kids, chasing big goals, and rebuilding a life on my terms. Most of the men I met weren't ready for that. Some were still figuring themselves out, others chasing their own dreams, and many weren't looking for someone with kids or a full life already in motion. And honestly...that was okay.

I didn't need to be chosen. I was already choosing myself. I wasn't waiting around—I was building something solid.

Meanwhile, the nanny who had once moved into my home? Yeah—no surprise—they were now officially dating. Was I shocked? Not even a little. From the beginning, I knew that the entire arrangement was just another manipulation tactic—something made to look innocent when it clearly wasn't. When someone can't be alone, not even for a month, that says a lot.

I'd seen the pattern before. I got pregnant, and suddenly we got a new car. He got separated, and suddenly he was dating beauty pageant girls, flying on jets, and living his best life. The divorce was finally over—business was booming, the image sparkling, girlfriend moved in—while no one really knew what was happening behind the scenes.

One of the hardest parts of abuse is watching the abuser seem to move on so quickly, as if their life only gets better. And there were moments I felt resentful. Not for what he had or the image he tried to maintain but because I was the one left doing all the hard work. I was literally in the trenches carrying a deep emotional weight, protecting my children from ongoing emotional, verbal, and mental abuse. I was in survival mode and trying to heal, not just move on with the next man.

I was left with the old version of the life *he* had created and the old version of *me* that came with it. Trying to heal, rebuild, and pick up all the broken pieces but picking up real momentum and thriving nonetheless.

My life was far from easy. I was still in survival mode most days, but I was working my ass off to create something better. Something real. All while chaos, toxicity, and criticism still circled around me.

RECLAIM YOURSELF

When I started fighting, the narrative shifted again. Suddenly it was, *I told you she was crazy,* or *She's unstable. She has issues.* He'd act curious around the kids, asking what I was doing, trying to gather information about me, pretending to be supportive, then turn around and send me emails tearing me down after my first loss. That I was a loser, a man, and I needed to get a real life.

The mind games, the harassment, and the demeaning language never stopped. I already knew what it all was: manipulation, control, and projection. But that didn't mean it didn't hurt and affect me.

I kept training because fighting and fitness became the best form of personal development I could've ever stumbled into. It kept me focused, healthy, and grounded in every area of my life.

When I started fighting, some people assumed I must've been angry or unstable, but it was actually the opposite. Fighting became the tool that helped me heal and grow. It taught me boundaries. It taught me how to continually stand up for myself, how to stay in my lane, and most importantly, it transformed me from the inside out.

My dad wasn't exactly thrilled about it. We butted heads for a long time about fighting because he didn't really understand what it was doing for me—not until much later. But even with his reservations, he tried to be supportive in his way. And I never backed down. I kept training. I kept saying yes to fights. Because I knew what it meant to me, even if no one else fully did yet.

Physically, I had always been strong, but in every other way, I was rebuilding from the ground up. Training to fight didn't just make me stronger; it became a shield. It kept the wrong people at a distance and protected the version of me that was still healing. It gave me back something I hadn't realized I'd lost: a voice. A sense of personal power that had been buried under years of silence and survival.

What surprised me most was how the gym—this gritty, intense, male-dominated space—turned out to be one of the safest places I'd ever known. I was surrounded by tough men, the kind who fought hard and trained harder, but they were also some of the kindest, most respectful people I'd ever met. They never tried to shrink or belittle me. Never made me feel small.

Instead, they pushed me to get better. They encouraged me when I wanted to quit. They saw my strength and helped me refine it. And that kind of steady, unspoken support? It meant more than they'll ever know. I'd spent so many years being torn down that I didn't even realize how much I needed to be built back up—until I was.

In between training, I still had to work. I had left my job working for the nurse practitioner and found a new opportunity at a funeral home. I know it might sound morbid, but hear me out. I was still very much trying to figure myself out, like most people in their twenties. I just happened to have a divorce under my belt and two kids while doing it.

I felt an undeniable pull toward funeral directing. I had always been fascinated by forensics, but after losing my brother, that calling grew stronger. What once was just an interest started to deepen into something more meaningful.

RECLAIM YOURSELF

It might sound strange or even heavy, but something about that experience stuck with me, especially the compassion and kindness shown by the man who helped guide our family through my brother's funeral. He was incredibly good at what he did, and in one of the worst moments of our lives, he made it feel just a little more bearable. That left a lasting impact on me and inspired me to consider helping others in the same way.

I started looking into funeral directing more seriously and eventually began taking classes while working at a local funeral home. The one I was drawn to was owned by a couple originally from California—young, vibrant, and nothing like the typical image of funeral directors. They brought a modern, compassionate, human energy to the space. They were just really cool. The female owner wore Chanel and Christian Louboutin's to pick ups.

One of my roles was doing transports, picking people up from homes, hospitals, morgues, and care centers, then bringing them back to be prepared for their service. It felt like sacred work. Through those experiences, I came to believe, without a doubt, that some people linger after they pass. I had always felt that with my brother, and working at the funeral home only confirmed it. There's a presence you can't quite explain. Not everyone sticks around, but some do. And when they do, you feel it.

One moment in particular has stayed with me. I was asked to meet the owner and swap Suburbans for a task. When I switched vehicles, I realized there was a body in the back. After returning to the funeral home and wheeling the black bag inside, I checked the paperwork—it was a young man who had passed just hours earlier from a drug overdose. And he was still there. His presence was strong, like he hadn't fully let go yet.

It wasn't scary. It was just real. The spirit is present and felt.

Moments like that completely shifted the way I viewed life, death, and everything in between. What started as a quirky job interest turned out to be exactly what I needed to help heal my spirit.

I was offering a heartfelt service to people in some of their most difficult moments, which helped me.

What I learned is that funeral directing is more than just a profession. It's a calling. These are people who dedicate their lives to being of service, answering calls at all hours, waking up in the middle of the night, and showing up with compassion, care, and grace every time.

I had started taking college classes to pursue a degree in funeral directing, but eventually, I realized I wasn't ready to commit my life fully to that path. Fighting was still calling to my soul.

Eventually, I found another job and moved on. But my time at the funeral home will always hold a special place in my heart. It gave me healing, purpose, and a deeper appreciation for the sacredness of life and death.

When my lease ended on the townhome, my parents stepped in once again to help me find a place, this time, one to buy. My oldest was heading into junior high, so we looked for something a bit closer to the school. We ended up finding a spot about fifteen minutes away, and my youngest switched to a charter school nearby. Once again, we settled in. This move felt more permanent, like it would be home for a while.

Around the same time, I found a new job—something with more structure, more consistency, and the kind of stability I'd been craving for a long time. It wasn't just about a paycheck; it was about rebuilding life on solid ground. Slowly but surely, things started falling into place.

Life kept moving, as it always does, and I kept moving with it—this time with more intention, clarity, and a deeper commitment to the life I was creating for my daughters and me. And for the first time in a long time, it wasn't about survival anymore. It was about building something beautiful, something lasting—something that felt like home.

A few months later, another fight opportunity came up, this time at a fitness convention. It felt full-circle in a way. I had spent years in that world, building relationships in the fitness industry. The job I had recently started was in the beauty space, and everything kind of connected. The company I was working for even had a booth at the expo I helped put together, and I was stepping into the cage to fight.

During that time, an up-and-coming influencer who also worked there followed me behind the scenes for a campaign I'd been asked to be part of. She had been a little upset that she wasn't selected, so I invited her to join me, gave her a behind-the-scenes look, and had her sit front row at the fights. The campaign centered around loss, specifically the loss of my brother and the journey of becoming a single mom.

One unexpected and deeply meaningful thing that came from sharing my story during this time was seeing the impact it had on others. The girl I connected with and brought to the behind the scenes and my fight was so moved by my experience—especially my journey with losing my brother to suicide—that she went on to create an entire brand inspired by it and her personal journey with mental health. Her message centered around the idea that it's a wonderful day to be alive. That phrase became her anchor, and eventually, her brand grew into something much bigger for her.

It felt amazing to know that my story had inspired something so meaningful.

There was also a female fighter who once told me to "stop being a victim" as she dismissed what healing looked like for me. At the time, it hurt—she misunderstood my journey and life completely.

But a few years later, she started doing the same thing with her own life.

It reminded me why I kept speaking up. Why did I keep healing out loud? Because even when people judge you, mock you, or talk shit—they're still watching.

First they'll criticize. Then they'll copy. And she did.

To have that kind of impact on someone else's life through my own pain and healing is beautiful to witness.

It's the kind of magic that changes people for the better: authentic, not controlling. Transformative, not toxic.

RECLAIM YOURSELF

And while a part of me still feels like my image and likeness were taken advantage of in both circumstances, I also recognize the meaning behind it. I had contributed something real, something personal, and it sparked someone else's purpose. If that's part of my purpose in this life, I'll own it.

That matters to me. And it always will.

And this next fight? It was different.

I chose a new walkout song, one that lit something up inside me. The kind of song that makes you feel like you're stepping into something bigger than yourself. The energy in the air was electric. I could feel the nerves creeping in as I stood behind the curtain, gloves on, heart pounding, trying to stay locked in. But underneath the nerves, there was this deep, grounded sense of confidence. I had trained harder. I felt stronger. I wasn't walking in unsure—I was walking in ready.

The support was overwhelming. The guys from the gym, my friends, my family—they were all there, cheering me on, believing in me. And this time, I believed in myself too.

As I stepped into the cage, the lights felt brighter, the crowd louder, but I was calmer. Focused. Ready.

The fight itself was more intense. Early on, she landed a stiff jab that broke my nose—blood poured the entire fight. But I didn't panic. I stayed composed, trusted my training, and kept pushing forward. I moved with more confidence, let my skills shine, and fought with everything I had at the time. I was still just a baby in the MMA world, but I was putting it all out there.

When the final bell rang, and they raised my hand in a unanimous decision, it wasn't just a win. It was a moment of redemption. A breakthrough. A reminder that I was exactly where I was supposed to be.

My family and kids came again, and it felt amazing to have their support. Winning felt better than losing, of course, but what meant the most was seeing all the pieces I'd been working on come together in the cage. That momentum fueled me. I kept training, working and, little by little, putting my life back together.

I was finally starting to feel like a whole person again, someone with options, freedom, and a future that wasn't dictated by someone else's control. I was creating autonomy, not falsely getting tangled in someone's web to create it.

Still Trying to Tear Me Down

You'd think my ex would've finally left me alone. It had been a few years now.

He had a girlfriend living with him, a growing business, and all the freedom he could ask for. But the more I succeeded, the more it seemed to bother him. He got more controlling and chaotic.

Instead of backing off, he became more difficult. Creating chaos through my children to try to gain control of my life.

RECLAIM YOURSELF

My kids started getting nervous to tell me what was going on at their dad's house. They'd been told more than once that what happens there stays there.

The yelling, the walking on eggshells, the tension—it was all still part of their monthly life.

The truth was, I just wasn't present to witness things the way I used to be. And whenever I did try to step in, it only created more tension for them. He would twist it into chaos and make it look like I was creating the problem or part of it. I absolutely wasn't. The only times I ever engaged with him were when I heard he was mistreating my girls, and they had no reason to lie about that.

But even that caused more harm than good for them.

Other than that, I wanted nothing to do with him. I didn't want to be involved in his life. If he would've married his girlfriend and left the state, I would've been ecstatic and grateful.

I would've signed off on that immediately.

I was the only one standing up for my children, the only one who knew how he really treated them at times. I stayed focused on their well-being, kept my distance, and didn't engage in drama, no matter how much I may have wanted to speak up at every incident. I made a conscious choice to stay out of the way and pour my energy into what I was building for us. I started focusing on educating them on abuse rather than constantly trying to stop it and point the finger. Letting them eventually see the truth for themselves. Meanwhile, he continued to weave a completely different narrative from the outside, one that couldn't have been further from the truth.

My heart ached watching my girls stuck in a cycle of emotional manipulation they never asked to be part of. They were caught in chaos that never should've been theirs to carry.

He traveled often, which on its own wasn't an issue. But our agreement was clear: If he couldn't be with the girls during his time, I had first right to have them. That rarely happened. He'd leave without telling me and have his girlfriend or family step in instead. It wasn't just frustrating—it hurt. It felt like he was trying to rewrite the story, one where I was the absent parent, that I cared more about fighting and myself when the reality was that I was always ready and wanting to be there.

When I couldn't due to work, I appreciated that his girlfriend—the same one who had once moved into my house—was kind to my daughters. In fact, she was an answer to a prayer that my kids would be cared for when I wasn't there.

That was never the issue. My girls knew I was grateful for that and for her, even though we didn't have a relationship.

The real issue was the dishonesty—the way the truth kept getting twisted. He made it look like I was prioritizing my life and dreams over my role as a mother when, in fact, I was never even given the chance. And every time it happened, I had to go out of my way to ask for time with my children. If you know anything about abuse, when they are falsely accusing you of something, it's most often a projection of how they are living.

This pattern continued. Over and over, the same manipulation, the same unfairness—my kids caught in the middle, not by accident but by design. And that was the hardest part of all.

I didn't speak much with his girlfriend. I knew he had spun a completely different story about why we divorced. And I knew that if I tried to speak up, I'd just be seen as the crazy ex-wife trying to stir up problems. But by that point, she had been around long enough to witness some of his outbursts and behavior firsthand. I told her more than once to step in and do something. She knew things weren't okay.

I don't know what she was able to do, if anything, but at some point, I had to let go and trust that my kids would grow up and be able to make informed choices about how much of a relationship they wanted with their dad. I had to trust them on that.

I had no control over what went on in that house, and I already knew how skilled he was at flipping the script. The hard part was knowing that he still provided a lifestyle that was hard to walk away from—especially when you're young and luxury feels like love and comfort. A lifestyle I very much should also be providing. A lifestyle I absolutely helped build, yet I was living much differently.

I kept their spirits strong, taught them uplifting coping tools, and encouraged them to build a spiritual relationship that brought them peace, which I knew they'd need to continually navigate their lives through chaos.

At the time, we were all trapped in one way or another—me by a divorce decree, them by their age and dependency. I couldn't fully provide for us, and I couldn't get them full time. We were doing the best we could, and I was doing all that I could to prepare them for when they could be independent.

When you're caught in ongoing mistreatment, it's known as Complex PTSD (C-PTSD). That's what we were living. Not every week was awful. We had fun days. Laughter. Good memories. But the undercurrent of abuse was always there.

I made sure they had access to therapy, someone outside of me they could talk to safely, just in case they were afraid of making things worse by being honest at home. They needed more safe spaces.

As a mother, it was heartbreaking to watch them carry that weight. I could see it in their eyes, the confusion, the quiet hurt they didn't always have the words for, feel it in the subtle tension between us at times. They were trying so hard to be strong, to make sense of a situation that never should've been theirs to navigate. And even though they rarely spoke about it, I knew they felt it all. What's even more confusing about all of it is the way coercive control puts a wedge between you and the people you love. It creates isolation, hardens your mindset and soul in ways you don't realize until you break free and aren't constantly surrounded by it.

There's a certain kind of pain that comes with watching your children suffer in silence—knowing you can't protect them from everything but wishing with all your heart you could.

RECLAIM YOURSELF

So I kept doing the work. I kept showing up—for myself and for them. I knew that the only way to lead them out of that cycle was to model something different. I couldn't erase the confusion they'd already experienced, but I could give them something better going forward: a steady example of what healing looks like, what self-respect sounds like, and what love should feel like.

More than anything, I wanted them to see that peace was possible. That they were allowed to have boundaries. That they didn't have to carry someone else's chaos just to keep the peace. I was determined to teach them, by the way I lived, that their voice matters—and so does their happiness.

Another few months passed, and I got a call about another fight. This time, I was going to Nebraska and then Florida for the biggest opportunity of my career so far.

Chapter 10

Heartbreak

I continued working, training, and spending time with my family. Still single as ever—but content with that. Life felt full in the ways that mattered. My nieces and nephew were growing up fast, and we all made an effort to carve out cousin time whenever we could. Sunday afternoons became our sacred space, slow, simple, and filled with laughter. Those quiet moments together reminded me of how healing it is just to be around people who love you without conditions and manipulation.

My girls were thriving—growing up quickly, excelling in basketball, keeping their grades strong, and doing their best to navigate the wild ride of adolescence with grace. There were more good days than not, and that alone felt like a small miracle. My parents continued to be the rock beneath all of it. Their love was constant, their presence unwavering. They showed up again and again. I will always be grateful for the way they held space for us, not just logistically but emotionally. They've been incredible grandparents and an anchor in my storm.

RECLAIM YOURSELF

At one point, I tried opening up to my family about the abuse enough to help them understand what I'd been carrying. But most of it didn't quite land. They didn't see it the way I did. All they saw was the surface, like most people. They had seen the smiling photos, the vacations, the appearances of success, and the charm he turned on so easily in public. Behind closed doors, it was very different. It's hard to explain a kind of harm that leaves no visible scars, especially when the person causing it knows how to make others feel special. He had a way of winning people over—organizing golf outings with my dad, spending time with my sister's family, and showing up with thoughtfulness and generosity. He could be incredibly fun, caring, charismatic, and kind. That version of him was real, too, which made it all the more confusing.

But just because someone can be loving in one moment doesn't mean they aren't harmful in another. That duality is what makes emotional abuse so difficult to name, let alone understand, especially from the outside looking in.

Eventually, I started setting boundaries. Not out of anger but out of necessity. Gentle at first, then more direct, as I realized how important it was to protect my peace. I started to name the behaviors for what they were. Gaslighting. Control. Emotional manipulation. I wanted my family to understand, not to place blame, but so we could create a safer emotional space for my daughters, especially during sports games and events where both sides of the family had to show up.

Even that felt impossible sometimes. I'd walk into a gymnasium and feel the tension the second I stepped out of the car. Glares in the parking lot. Forced smiles. Loud voices echoing from the stands. He'd yell at the refs, try to insert himself into the coaching, and draw all the attention to himself as if the game was about him. Meanwhile, I was just trying to sit quietly and watch my daughters play a sport, pretending the air around me wasn't heavy with unresolved conflict.

I smiled anyway. For as long as I could. For them.

Because they deserved that—joy, pride, and peace on the sidelines, even if I had to fight for it in silence.

Eventually, I reached a point where I couldn't pretend anymore. I couldn't keep smiling through it, couldn't keep making it all look easy. And just like that, I became the problem again, the one causing tension, and the one making things messy.

But I wasn't creating chaos—I was just no longer willing to stay silent in it. I was finally speaking up, setting boundaries, and choosing honesty over appearances. And to some, that looked like drama.

To me, it looked like growth.

Fight News and High School Basketball

When fight offers come in, there's always a pause, a moment where you have to weigh your options. Does this opponent make sense for me? Can I win this fight? What's their style? How do I match up? And more importantly, what skills and aspects of my fight game do I need to sharpen to come out on top?

RECLAIM YOURSELF

This particular opponent was also a striker. Based on what I'd seen, I felt confident. I'd been logging hours at the gym, putting in serious work, and mentally, I was in a solid place. So I accepted. I was ready and genuinely excited. Nervous but still excited!

I did everything right. Made weight. Showed up to weigh-ins. Dialed in, focused. But then. . .she didn't show. And when she finally did? She was ten pounds over.

Ten. Pounds. Over.

That's not just an off day. That's a completely different fight.

I had a choice right then to walk away or fight anyway. And technically, I had every right to decline. But I'd already done the hard part: the prep, the weight cut, the travel, the mindset work. I wasn't walking away. I didn't come this far to stop outside the cage.

So I said yes. Fully aware of the risk. Because ten pounds *matters*. It changes everything: speed, power, durability. It changes how you get hit. And believe me, I felt it. My face definitely felt it!

Her shots were heavy. Heavier than I expected. Every punch carried more weight, and my face took the damage to prove it. My forehead swelled. I left with a solid black eye, giant forehead lumps, and bruises down the side of my shoulder and arm from the cage, but I also left with the win, and that felt good! I had a teammate also fighting on that card, and he won too. It was a great night for our fight gym!

This fight taught me a lot. I needed more head movement, no question. But I also proved something to myself: I could still choose courage. I could bet on myself. Even when the odds shifted at the last minute, I didn't fold. I stood up and fought, and I won.

Each fight teaches you something you can't learn anywhere else. This time, it was about overcoming fear, trusting myself more, and following through on my word. That gave me momentum. That gave me confidence. And I absolutely needed both.

That win wasn't just about the fight.

It was about reclaiming a part of me I thought I had lost for good.

In addition to my fight stuff, my fitness journey was growing too. I was offered a chance to contribute to a fitness magazine, a big opportunity. I said yes without hesitation. Ironically, it was easier for me to talk about suicide than it was to talk about everything else I was still walking through. Hardly anyone knew what I'd been enduring all those years in my marriage and divorce.

But writing about mental health and how fitness and fighting helped keep my mind strong came naturally. I poured truth into those pieces, and people felt it.

I had earned several certifications in community suicide prevention and mental health awareness. I became a certified personal trainer and yoga teacher. I helped organize events, spoke at fundraisers, and began aligning myself with causes that mattered deeply to me.

Because I knew, both in and out of the cage, I wasn't just fighting to win matches. I was fighting to heal, to grow, to lead. I was fighting for my life and for the lives of others too.

RECLAIM YOURSELF

Getting published in mainstream media was a huge moment, not just for me personally but for the message I was trying to share around suicide prevention and finding an uplifting gym routine or movements. How moving your body not only helps you physically but mentally too. One of the articles I wrote was about the gym being a lifeline for people battling depression and suicidal thoughts. That issue featured Ryan Reynolds on the cover, and seeing my words printed in that same publication felt like another win, one that meant something.

The more space I put between myself and the chaos I had lived through, the more genuine, aligned opportunities started to show up. Slowly, I was watching the life I'd always believed was possible unfold, and it felt real, not like it was going to be taken away from me.

I brought my daughters with me to Barnes & Noble to pick up the issue, and that moment meant the world to me, even if they didn't fully understand why. After everything we'd been through, having them witness even a small moment of success felt like a big deal.

I was grateful they got to see me experience joy and accomplishment, especially in a way that was meaningful and rooted in purpose. After so much confusion and pain, that win felt different. It was raw. It was earned. And it marked the beginning of something new for me. The small wins were starting to stack up, and for the first time in a long time, the pace of life was shifting in a hopeful direction.

Then the incident with my daughter happened.

As a parent, especially one who'd had a child young, it was hard to process. You know these things can happen. My daughter has free will, and I respect that, especially because I have a strong will, but it's never what you want for your child.

And what came next was even more painful than anything I'd previously experienced.

She was dating a football player and still very young and figuring out life. It was her first relationship. They dated for more than a few months and chose to be physically intimate.

And when her dad found out they were sexually active, he lost it. Pulled her out of school without me knowing, degraded her, spit his gum in her face, slapped her, choked her, called her names no father should ever say, and continued to torment her for days after in a non-physical but more damaging way. When she told me what had happened, I broke. I pulled her close, wrapped her in the biggest hug I could give, and reminded her of what every daughter deserves to hear:

This is not your fault. You don't deserve this.

No father should ever treat his daughter that way, no matter what choices she's making in her life.

She was a straight-A student, a dedicated athlete, kind-hearted, and a beautiful person inside and out. She didn't deserve to be shamed, degraded, assaulted, or made to feel small.

And yet, that's exactly what happened. What he got away with—again.

Only this time, it escalated.

RECLAIM YOURSELF

This time, it crossed a line.

It was abuse. And it had turned physical. He had put his hands on her—choked her.

If you know anything about abuse, you know strangulation is extremely serious. It's one of the most dangerous forms there is. It's not just about force—it's about control. About taking someone's power, their safety, their breath—and putting it in the hands of someone who's trying to dominate them.

Whether it lasts two seconds or ten, the message is the same: *I own you. I can take everything from you.*

He could try to downplay it all he wanted, but the truth was undeniable, and that won't ever change.

No father should ever put his hands on his daughter—or any woman. I don't care how extravagant the trips are, how many shopping sprees he takes her on, what kind of car she drives, or how comfortable the lifestyle is. I don't care how kind, caring, protective, understanding, or "cool" he can be on his good days—or if she forgives him.

None of that erases the damage. None of it makes it okay. Period.

And hearing that from her shattered me. My stomach dropped. I couldn't believe we were here.

I never imagined he'd treat our children this way. I should've known better. It always turns physical.

I called my attorney right away. She told me to report it, so I did. I called the local police department in the city where it happened, shared every detail I could, and filed the report. But I wasn't physically there. For anything to move forward, she had to speak up too.

And she was terrified. Not just of the process but of the aftermath. She still had to go back to his house. She still had to figure out how to navigate a relationship that wasn't always physically abusive but was always laced with control and confusion.

And then came the gaslighting.

He knew people in law enforcement and planted the seed and belief that nothing she did or I did would matter. And to me, that is one of the most dangerous kinds of abuse there is—when someone is made to feel like their voice, their truth, and their safety don't matter. With the previous domestic violence charge, he would've gotten another charge, possibly jail time, a felony. Child abuse is no joke. He was working overtime to cloud her mind and silence her, and sadly, it worked.

What could she do? He'd made her feel hopeless, powerless, and downplayed his physical harm. He wouldn't have done that if she didn't do what she did.

That weekend she stayed with me. It was my time with her. But the fear lingered. I had always been uneasy sending them back to him—but this? This was different. This felt paralyzing. And yet, I couldn't legally keep them with me. Not without her filing her statement.

RECLAIM YOURSELF

I had voiced my concerns for years—the yelling, the manipulation, the intimidation. I had tried to step in whenever I could and knew when it was happening. But emotional abuse so often slips through the cracks, especially post-divorce. Unless there are physical injuries that are clearly reported and followed through with, it's dismissed.

Even now, even with physical harm involved, the burden was still on her to speak. And she was just a teenager, caught in the middle of fear, loyalty, and confusion.

And yet again, I was back in that familiar place. The one where I tried to name what was happening. The one where I stood alone, where I was seen as the problem, as if I was overreacting or fueling drama. When all I ever did was say: *This isn't love. This isn't normal. Healthy men don't treat women and girls this way. Why is no one stopping this?*

And still, I carried the weight—because someone had to. Because their emotional well-being mattered more than anyone's comfort. Because I was their mother.

I kept training. Kept working. Kept showing up.

Even when I was running on fumes. Even when the grief and exhaustion felt like too much. I stayed grounded in one truth: that if I kept going, if I kept healing, then maybe—*just maybe*—when the time came, when my girls were grown, safe, and thriving. . .

I'd get to thrive too. And that eventually? I was still holding onto it. Still building it. One quiet, steady, soul-strong step at a time.

The Fight Gym

The fight gym became one of the safest, most healing spaces in my life, even when others didn't understand it. My dad hated it. He'd often try to talk me out of it, not entirely out of control but out of concern. He didn't fully see what it was doing for me. What he couldn't quite grasp was that being there was giving me back something I hadn't had in a long time—boundaries, strength, and a sense of ownership over my body and my choices.

It was one of the few places where men weren't trying to control me or define me. They were uplifting me and helping me get stronger.

When you start choosing a different path, especially one that doesn't fit the mold, it tends to make people uncomfortable. Even the well-meaning ones. I'd heard the analogy before: crabs in a barrel. When one crab tries to climb out, the others pull it back down. Not always out of malice but because it disrupts what feels familiar or safe to them. And part of my growth was learning to recognize that...and keep climbing anyway.

I had to start trusting my intuition again, something that had been dismissed, gaslit, or overruled for far too long. Choosing a path that others didn't understand required me to stand firmly in what *felt* right for *me*, even when it didn't make sense to *them*.

I got plenty of pushback. Side comments. Power struggles, attitude, and envy. Questions I didn't always have answers for. But I kept showing up. My groundwork still pushed me outside my comfort zone, but slowly, it started to make sense. I even began looking forward to grappling. The movements, the muscle memory, the rhythm of it all, it started to click.

My girls kept showing up, game after game, practice after practice. They were growing stronger, more skilled, and more confident with every season. Watching them progress in basketball, put in the work, and find their rhythm is something I'll never take for granted. I kept showing up too. I was training, working, healing, and doing everything I could to support not just their growth but my own.

I couldn't always give them everything financially. Their dad had more money and access to extra resources, and he made sure they had private lessons, top-tier training, summer camps, and all the gear they could ever need. And to his credit, he always showed up in this way. He made time for nearly every game, covered expenses, and stayed actively involved in their basketball journey—and that matters. I'll never take that away from him.

I've also learned that presence and paying for everything doesn't always equal support.

Because when things didn't go perfectly—when they had an off game, made mistakes, or didn't meet his expectations—the pressure would mount. The criticism would come in heavy, increasing the emotional weight of needing to perform just right or face his disappointment and berating.

It wasn't about nurturing their growth. It was about control. About perfection.

He had never played at the level they were already reaching. Yet there he was, shouting from the sidelines, micromanaging every move, putting his own identity into their performance. Behind closed doors, it became even more confusing—praise mixed with put-downs, support tangled with stress. My youngest took the brunt of his expectations, especially after my oldest graduated high school and moved on to college ball. More often than not, she got mother fucked after games, practices, or even something as simple as getting a flat tire on her car. His emotional, verbal, and mental abuse was constant. Relentless. She grew less forgiving over time and started setting boundaries—especially after high school basketball ended.

The most confusing part was that basketball had always been *their* connection. It was how her father bonded with her. So when she put boundaries around it, part of that connection broke—and that loss hurt.

It was pain she didn't cause and never deserved.

Once again, all of us were hurting because of one person's refusal to change.

It was a double-edged sword; they learned to live with it, survive it. Because basketball was *his* dream for them for most of their lives. His manipulative way of handling basketball, his daughter, and his role as a father was a mix of inconsistency and verbal, emotional, and mental abuse—always followed by grand gestures after the poor treatment. That was his pattern. The only difference was my daughters were just children. Teenagers. Trying to make sense of it all while carrying the weight of someone else's unresolved life.

RECLAIM YOURSELF

And while I didn't have a say in what happened at his house or much say in the direction of their basketball journey—he was the one steering that ship—I did what I could. I stayed grounded in love. I reminded them of their worth beyond performance.

I stayed focused on our home being a place of peace, not pressure.

They kept their head in the game, found their own motivation, and let their work speak for itself. And I'm endlessly proud of them for that.

They won two high school championships. Two! Players of the game, highlight reels, trophies, rings—the whole thing. It was incredible to witness.

But even more than the medals and celebrations, what mattered most was the pride in their eyes. They knew what it took to earn that moment.

It was theirs. Not their dad's.

And just as they were reaching that milestone, I got a call that would become a milestone of my own.

It felt surreal—but somehow, not surprising. Deep down, I had a gut feeling the call would come someday. It didn't happen for everyone, but I *knew* it would happen for me. My parents never bought in; fighting was always a source of slight tension. Just get a real job.

After years of grinding in the gym, pushing through discomfort, juggling motherhood, rebuilding my life, and healing parts of myself I thought were broken—I was finally being invited to do something I had only dreamed about: my first professional MMA fight.

It wasn't just a shot at the cage. It was a moment that reflected every ounce of work I had put in behind the scenes—through every season of struggle, every setback, every small win that no one else saw.

This wasn't luck. It was earned.

I wasn't entirely prepared to fight at that level—at least not on paper—but I answered the call, anyway. Because something in my soul was stirring, it wasn't just about stepping into the cage. It was about stepping into a version of myself I had fought so hard to become.

An invitation to step into the cage and take my first professional MMA fight on a major platform.

It wasn't glamorous. It wasn't for fame. It wasn't for money.

It was for *me.*

It was about honoring the woman I had become. The one who refused to give up. The one who kept showing up—in the gym, in court, at school drop-offs, and tournaments—no matter how tired, how hurt, or how stretched thin.

It was about stepping into more of me.

So when that call came, I didn't hesitate.

Because I knew this was more than a fight. It was a beginning.

Professional Athlete Status

I was at Target, casually running errands before my youngest's final high school basketball game—just soaking in those last sweet moments of her senior year—when the text came in.

Then the call.

It was the matchmaker.

My heart picked up before I even answered. He asked if I could be ready. *Show up. Make weight. Be the alternate.* No promises. Just *be ready.*

I'd been training, sure. But my focus had been on my girls, not preparing for war. And now, I had twelve days to flip the switch—to grind harder than I ever had, lock in, and push my body and mind to fight shape.

I did just that.

I flew out to Florida. Did the paperwork. Passed the physicals. Showed up to weigh-ins. I made weight. Still. . .nothing. No green light. No opponent. Just waiting, thinking I was going to enjoy a relaxing few days in Florida.

Until the text came through.

You're fighting.

My stomach flipped.

Then came the second part: She's an Olympic wrestling qualifier. Just crossed over to MMA.

I stared at my phone.

Out of all the matchups on the card—this was the toughest draw possible.

The worst-case scenario. A heavy grappler. Olympic-level wrestling pedigree.

Exactly the kind of opponent most strikers avoid, especially me because I was still trudging through my ground work. I was definitely not at that level of grappling yet.

Chapter 11
Professional Athlete Status

I stayed calm and collected because what else could I do? I wasn't prepared for this opponent in the traditional sense. I hadn't trained specifically for her. I hadn't even known I'd be fighting, so I hadn't game-planned the way I usually would. But in so many other ways, I was more prepared than I gave myself credit for. Like so many moments in my life before, when I took that pregnancy test at sixteen, when I got the call that my brother had taken his life, when I stood in that funeral home and saw him for the last time, when I walked into court to fight for what was mine to survive, a quiet calm came over me. A surreal kind of stillness. This moment carried that same weight. It was big and overwhelming, and yet I stepped into it.

Like I mentioned earlier, part of fighting is learning to let go of your ego. I already knew this wasn't going to go my way. Not in a "poor me" kind of way. And no matter how many mindset tools I knew how to utilize, I knew the odds weren't in my favor. And choosing to step into something knowing you'll likely lose? That's a whole different kind of courage. I'd been practicing that for years.

The next morning came the media weigh-ins. I showed up, made weight, and faced off with my opponent. I could see the nerves in her eyes and her shaking hands, but I didn't get it twisted; she was tough as hell. A female electrician, a former cop, and a lifelong wrestler. That basically tells you everything you need to know. Wrestling is one of the hardest, most relentless disciplines in MMA. This was her pro debut, and she had every edge, months of focused training, the right prep, and the right camp. The hype. More experience in a few areas.

And there I stood. No excuses, no backup plan. Just me, grounded in everything I'd already survived. I was ready to face whatever came head on. I smiled for the cameras, gathered my gear, and headed back to my room to refuel and relax.

I went to sleep that night feeling excited but still a bit disconnected from myself. There were parts of me that hadn't fully caught up to the moment, parts still frozen in old memories, old patterns, and old versions of life that had shaped me. My mind would drift, tugging me back to what was, even as I tried to stay present in what *was happening now*. I was doing something huge, achieving my dream of becoming a professional athlete. I just never expected that dream to look like stepping into a cage to fight someone.

And that was something I was incredibly proud of. After everything I'd walked through— grief, abuse, and rebuilding a life from the ground up—I had made it here. Living it. Owning it. Becoming the fighter I knew I had in me all along. Reclaiming everything that tried to erode these parts of me since I was fifteen years old.

What I came to realize is that resilience is at the core of what it means to be a fighter. You don't have to step into a cage and fight professionally to want the qualities a fighter has—grit, strength, mental toughness, and heart. Everyone wants that kind of resilience. And for me, it wasn't just something I was born with—it was something God planted in me and I've had to cultivate over time.

I know that because I had so many chances to quit, not just as an athlete but as a person. But I didn't. Every fight, every setback, every challenge was teaching me how to build resilience—not just in the gym but in life. It became a skillset I was constantly sharpening because life demanded it. I wanted to be present for my life instead of just surviving it. I was in the middle of my unique process to learn to be resilient.

I woke up the next day, ate breakfast, and packed everything I needed for the fight, which was the fight kit they provided and my mouth piece. I'd had my hair already braided the day before with a few of the other girls. All of us were shuttled over to the arena, and I sat alongside the other women fighting on the card, some of the fiercest women I've ever met. There's something uniquely powerful about being surrounded by female fighters. It's a rare kind of strength, a quiet knowing, and an unspoken bond you don't often find elsewhere, even if you're opponents.

That part? That part was fun.

CAMEE ADAMS

The shuttle ride was about twenty minutes, and when we pulled up, I stepped off and into the arena.

Before fights, you have two corners. You are in one area, and the opponents are in another area. The fights have an order, and you warm up in designated corners until it's your time to fight. I cracked pads, hit sprawls, stretched, and stayed focused with my coach.

Jeremy Horn, my longtime coach from Utah, was in my corner, and that brought a sense of familiarity in the unfamiliarity. Still, something about this fight was different. The energy in the air, the weight in my chest all felt heavier, different than usual. I wasn't as prepared for that as I wanted to be and took note of this feeling. Usually, before a fight, I'd feel a mix of nerves, anxiety, and fear but still connected to myself. This time was different. I felt calm...but disconnected. Like I wasn't fully in my body and mind. I didn't have a clear game plan in mind, and that was a mistake on my end. My mind felt blank like I was walking into my first fight all over again.

They announced my name, "Fighting out of the blue corner, Camee Double Whammy Adams," and I made the slow walk from the warm up area to the cage. The cut man put vaseline on my brow bones, nose, and chin. I showed my mouth piece, took a deep breath, looked into the cage, walked up the steps, and stepped in—for what would be the biggest moment of my fight career.

My adrenaline surged. My heart pounded. I stood in my corner while my opponent made her walk and entered the cage to her corner. We were brought up to the middle of the cage, touched gloves, and walked back to our sides of the cage.

RECLAIM YOURSELF

Then the bell rang, and the ref signaled for the fight to start.

With her being a lifetime wrestler, I knew she was going to take me down. I just didn't expect it to happen that fast. I should've started slower and been more calculated. I had more stand up experience than her, which was my only edge. But instead, I met her in the middle and threw a half-hearted jab-cross that lacked any real purpose. She slipped under it like it was nothing and bulldozed me straight into the cage.

We clinched for a second. I threw a few body shots, trying to buy time, trying to feel something click, but she was already two steps ahead. She got me to the ground, landed some hard hammer fists and ground and pound on the side of my face. The moment I turned my back, I knew I was screwed. She locked in the rear naked choke, and I made a split-second decision: I wasn't tapping. Not after taking the fight on short notice, not after everything I'd pushed through just to show up. I'd rather go out than give in.

And I did, I went out. Limp. Eyes rolled back. Spread eagle. It looked brutal. Way worse than it felt. The fight was over.

When I came to, I was smiling. Laughing even. The refs were waving their hands in front of my face, asking if I knew where I was. In my mind? I was back at Target shopping. Blacked out but oddly at peace. I stood up, walked back to my corner, and waited for the ref to call us back out to the middle to announce the winner. I was genuinely happy for her. I knew she'd go on to have a good professional career, and she did. I walked away with something too. Not a win but a deeper respect for the cage and what it demands. I walked out with respect for myself and what I'm capable of stepping up for and enduring, even in the face of fear, doubt, and risk. The fight ended in the first round. Not exactly my proudest moment, but it happens. Every fighter loses. It's part of the game. It still sucks to be on someone else's highlight reel.

I was proud of myself for showing up, even with how it ended.

I walked out of the cage, knowing it wasn't pretty. That kind of loss sticks with you, not because I didn't fight hard but because I knew I could've done better. I took my check, sat through the rest of the card like a pro, and kept my chin up. No meltdown. No victim story. Just a quiet reckoning with myself.

Back at the hotel, I packed up, stood under the shower, letting the heat hit my bruises, iced my face, and called it a night.

I woke up to a swollen temple, but honestly? I felt okay. Getting put to sleep in the first round meant I didn't take much damage, physically, at least. Emotionally, I'd have to process it later.

I caught my early flight and landed. My oldest daughter picked me up from the airport, and we headed home. I was still worn down from the fight, mentally and physically, but the second I walked through the door, I shifted gears because that's what moms do. Business as usual. Mom hat on. Fight behind me. I wasn't about to let one bad night stop the momentum I'd fought so hard to build.

My youngest had her heart set on going to Las Vegas to watch the women's NCAA basketball tournament. And despite being utterly exhausted after fifteen grueling days of training, cutting weight, traveling across the United States, and taking a tough loss, I didn't hesitate.

RECLAIM YOURSELF

The very next morning, we packed up and hit the road. Five hours to Vegas, just the two of us, making memories. I may have been running on fumes, but that's what moms do, and I knew she wanted to go. So we did.

Chapter 12

Where We Are Now

My oldest daughter graduated first, and two years later, my youngest followed. Watching them walk across those stages filled me with a pride I couldn't quite put into words. These weren't just academic achievements—they were deeply emotional moments. Each step they took felt like a chain breaking, releasing me from a life where I had been tethered through a legal agreement for far too long. For the first time in nearly two decades, I felt a deeper level of freedom—one I had longed for. A life truly separate from their father.

My oldest went on to earn a basketball scholarship while pursuing her bachelor's in nursing, showing grit, heart, and dedication every step of the way. Not long after, my youngest received her own scholarship to play in California, where she earned her business degree. She later accepted an offer to continue playing at a larger NCAA-accredited college in Washington.

After my youngest moved, I made a choice—I moved to Las Vegas. Not to escape or chase distraction but to explore life outside of the

RECLAIM YOURSELF

toxic bubble I'd been stuck in. Las Vegas was in the middle, close enough to both of them. To finally step out of the toxic environment I had endured for eighteen years. I could start fresh, in a place where no one knew my story—and everything aligned. Out of nowhere, I was offered a position at a new personal training gym, so at least I had a job there. To this day, I still don't know how they found me, but it felt like divine timing.

I bounced around for a bit, renting rooms that weren't exactly ideal, but they gave me a place to land. I visited my daughter in California often throughout her three years there, especially at the beginning when she didn't know anyone and was starting completely over. My oldest stayed surrounded by friends and family, so I knew she had a strong support system while I worked to rebuild mine.

The original plan was to train full-time and continue pursuing my dream of fighting professionally. I had landed in the fight capital of the world, surrounded by world-class coaches and inspiring female fighters. But something felt different. I was exhausted—not just in my body but in my spirit. Maybe it wasn't for me anymore. Maybe it was the accumulation of years spent pushing through survival. Whatever it was, my adrenal system was depleted. And for the first time in a long time, I let myself rest. I let myself let everything go to see what would stick.

Fighting takes a toll on every part of you, and I had been running on empty for years—raising daughters, surviving trauma, working, training, and doing everything without emotional support. My body needed a break. My soul did too. I had been fighting for so long and not just in MMA.

I shifted gears. I enrolled in college classes and began working toward my bachelor's degree—right alongside my daughters. I still trained a few times a week, but pulling together a full fight camp just wasn't realistic at the time. In fact, I was offered a big fight in London—an incredible opportunity I seriously considered—but something didn't feel quite right. She was an extremely decorated boxer coming over to MMA, and I'd seen this style of fight before. She was far past my level in striking, and I wasn't at one hundred percent. If I was going to step back into the cage, I knew I had to show up and win. I didn't want to take another loss just for the sake of saying I did it.

Instead, I chose to focus on school and another project that had been tugging at my heart—creating something of my own. I poured my energy into building my wellness brand rooted in mitt work and resilience. It started small but grew into something truly special. Over time, I hosted more than thirty events and watched this passion project turn into something fulfilling, impactful, and completely mine.

My oldest had an incredible basketball career, and somewhere in the midst of it all, she met the love of her life—the kind of partner I had always prayed she'd find. He treats her with unwavering kindness, deep respect, and the kind of care that allows her to feel safe enough to soften. To breathe. To rest in love instead of fighting for it.

Watching her experience that kind of steady, healthy love filled my heart in ways I didn't even know I needed. Her wedding was beautiful, joyful, and full of meaning—and a moment I'll never forget. Standing by her side as a proud mother, I felt this quiet sense of peace settle in. The weight I had carried for so many years, the protective armor I never took off—it started to lift.

A part of me came back that day.

Because I knew...she was safe now.

My youngest went on to earn her bachelor's in business and is now working toward her master's from a Big Ten school. She's focused, driven, and surrounded by good people—building a life that's both peaceful and powerful, entirely on her own terms. Like most young adults chasing big goals, she's stressed, but she's thriving, and I couldn't be more proud. She's also experienced loving, respectful relationships—ones built on trust and kindness—and I'm deeply grateful she's felt safe and valued in that way.

That's what I always dreamed of for my daughters: not just outward success but a deep sense of fulfillment. A life where they know their worth, walk in confidence, and feel supported as they grow. I can't wait to see where her journey leads next. The sky isn't just the limit—it's the starting line.

And me? I'm still single—and for the first time in my life, I'm not in survival mode. I became a certified personal trainer, yoga teacher, professional MMA fighter, earned my degree in communications with a minor in substance abuse counseling, launched a foundation focused on helping people and youth develop healthy coping skills, landed a feature story and cover spot I once only dreamed of—and, of course, I wrote this book.

These past few years, I have been healing, rebuilding, and learning to take up space without apology. I don't shrink to keep the peace anymore. I no longer feel the need to prove my worth—I live from a place of knowing it.

If life surprises me with love again, I'll welcome it. It's not that I don't want a relationship—I just haven't found one that lets me stay fully myself. And until that happens, I'm perfectly okay right here.

My parents are still incredible—almost retired now. My dad still loves his golf games and trips to the gym and has recently gotten into investing. My mom is the same salt-of-the-earth woman she's always been. She spends her days being the most thoughtful grandma, working, cooking, reading, and serving others. She worked tirelessly for years until she felt I was truly stable. She's supported me in every season of my life, and my dad has too. I'll never be able to thank them enough.

My sister and her family are doing well, thriving in their own way and living life to the fullest! Her kids are growing up, and I'm excited to see what they do next.

When I'm home, I always visit my brother's grave. He's still with me—in quiet moments, in signs often seen not just by me. There's an unshakable bond we'll always share. He's shown up for me in ways that are impossible to ignore, and I carry him with me always.

I'm endlessly grateful to everyone who has shown me love, kindness, healing and opportunities over the past decade. It's meant more to me than anyone will ever know. I handled the past twenty two years the best I knew how. It's only my first living. I wasn't perfect, but I did all that I could to thrive and circumstances that were meant to keep me small.

And you can make it through your hard things too. I promise.

If you've made it this far in my story, I hope it reminds you of your own strength. That you can endure, heal, and rebuild. Being strong and gritty for a moment will get you through a challenge—but learning to be resilient? That's what will carry you through life.

I hope my next book is filled with more light—with stories of what came after the storm.

More peace. More joy. More of the life I fought so hard to create.

Because that's the beautiful part of surviving: eventually, you get to live.

Really live. And that's the story I'm still writing.

Acknowledgements

To my beautiful family, especially my parents, thank you for loving me through every season. Your quiet strength and resilience helped me through the hardest years of my life until I could consistently stand on my own two feet. I am forever grateful.

To my brother who's never left my side, even after he went physically from this earth.

To everyone who lifted me up, whether knowingly or unknowingly. Thank you.

To my daughters, who watched me survive before they could watch me thrive, I love you more than words will ever hold. I wish healing had come faster!

You deserved a childhood filled with peace, safety, and joy, not the invisible weight of coercive control and confusion.

You deserved to see what healthy love looks like.

RECLAIM YOURSELF

And I deserved to live it too. I hope you saw what rebuilding yourself can look like, and you're able to reclaim it yourself.

You are loved tremendously.

To anyone reading this who feels stuck in a cycle of abuse, coercion, manipulation, or survival, please hear me:

You are not alone. You are not broken. You are not powerless, even when it feels like you are.

Leaving is hard. The longer you stay, the more entangled you become. But it is never too late to choose yourself. To reclaim your voice, your calm. To begin again.

Yes—it will hurt. Yes—it will be unfair. Yes—it will be one of the hardest things you'll ever do.

But it is your responsibility to save yourself. No one else can do it for you. You don't have to stay out of guilt or obligation. You don't have to keep mistaking pain for passion. You don't have to lose yourself, piece by piece, to keep someone else whole. Love should never cost you your soul.

You are allowed to leave. You are allowed to rebuild. You are allowed to create a life that feels safe, peaceful, and real.

If there's one thing I've learned, it's this: The peace, freedom, and clarity you long for? They are on the other side of the pain—and worth every step it takes to get there.

You are worth the fight.

With love, gratitude, and peace,

Camee

www.ingramcontent.com/pod-product-compliance
Lightning Source LLC
Chambersburg PA
CBHW030319080526
44584CB00012B/629